A QUEST WITHIN

by

Len Marshall

Published under licence from Andrews UK

With thanks to Annette for making this all possible.

To all the people who helped me make my book a reality.

Do not store up for yourselves treasures on earth, where moth and rust destroy, and where thieves break in and steal. But store up for yourselves treasures in heaven, where moth and rust do not destroy, and where thieves do not break in and steal. For where your treasure is, there your heart will be also.

Matthew 6:19

Chapter One

Whether you think you can or whether you think you cannot, either way you are right.

Henry Ford

Although they had met before, to her this was a special date. It was not that perfecting her make-up and hair and choosing the right outfit took so much time or indeed needed so much time, she had just become preoccupied with imagining how the evening would go and visualizing how she could achieve the successful result she sought. She had become distracted during her usually methodical preparations. Their reservation at a well-known city centre restaurant had already been made by her boyfriend who was on his way to pick her up. They had become friends through a dating website only a few weeks ago.

Their table was in a corner, where the diffused light threw a romantic subdued hue. As always, the man gazed appreciatively at the young woman who sat opposite him while she fixed her gaze upon the table and fiddled with her fork as if not listening to him, thinking of something else entirely.

Soon dinner was served and, while talking to him, she began to think about her next step, crucial for the completion of the evening's objective. They chatted throughout the meal, sometimes laughing, sometimes smiling. Now they were talking about their likes and dislikes in other people.

"I believe that it is our subconscious which defines our true personality," she said when they had finished their meal.

He was intrigued by her remarks "Well, what about our subconscious?"

"Very important but that does not define our true personality," she replied, looking at the waiter who was approaching the table with their bill. He would reach their table soon enough but all she needed was fifteen seconds to complete her task.

"And your views are based on what?" he was still trying to understand her reply.

She had anticipated this obvious question. Now was the time for her to act. She took a deep breath and pointed towards a couple sitting two tables away behind him. "What do you think about those two? Do you think they are lovers pretending to be friends?"

He turned his head to look behind at the table she had indicated. He took a brief look. That was all she had needed to distract him and now that his attention was elsewhere, she made her move. She picked up his mobile from the table, quietly shifting it under the table where she was already holding another phone of the exact make and model in her other hand. She put them together and it just took fifteen seconds before both phones were cloned completely.

"Well, what can I say? How can anyone say anything about the true relationship of two complete strangers?" he protested whilst turning round to face her again. He was perplexed by her reaction. She had a very mischievous smile on her face and her beautiful eyes were glowing excitedly even in the dimmed light. He suddenly became curious trying to figure out what was going on there.

"Subconscious," she said, whilst laughing, "There's nothing wrong with those two people Neil but my little experiment just tells me that you're a very curious person and take life a little too seriously." She was clearly teasing him.

"Clarke," he said her name a little louder as he realised she had started this conversation just to tease him. Although he appreciated her sense of humour, he also felt a little embarrassed. The waiter had reached their table with the bill. Whilst Neil was dealing with it, she put a phone back on the table. It was the one she had brought with her. Now both phones held the exact same data and contact records. Only the one on the table contained something else as well as its memory card.

"Don't worry sweetheart," Clarke continued, "it makes two of us. Look, I've already accepted what is wrong with my subconscious." This made Neil laugh then they both laughed together.

They left the restaurant and Neil dropped Clarke off at her place. As soon as she went in, she took her phone out and launched a tracking application which was now indicating a blinking red dot slowly moving away from her location. A big smile broke on her face. Neil was completely clueless about what had happened and unaware that his life in the coming days was about to be turned upside down.

***

The meeting was taking place in an abandoned warehouse located just outside the Queens' district in an isolated area on the outskirts of New York City. Absolute secrecy had to be maintained and everyone had travelled there individually pretending that they were alone. They were amongst the three most powerful men from China visiting the USA. One was the Chinese ambassador's assistant from the Chinese based in Washington. The second was a representative of the Political-Bureau. The third was one of China's senior Intelligence Chiefs.

This was not the first time they had met. In an earlier meeting, held four months ago in China, they had discussed their plans at a strategic level and it was concluded that they would have to find local help in order for their plan to succeed. Now the three collaborators were waiting for a fourth, the local contact. The plan presented by the Intelligence Chief had been considered excellent as a way by which to prevent the US Navy's maritime dominance in the Eastern Pacific Rim and particularly in the South China Sea.

"I hope this place is safe," said Wu Chin, the Chinese representative of the Political-Bureau.

"It is. We own it through an umbrella company as a cover for an oil subsidiary business" said Jinn Wu, the ambassador's assistant.

"So what's the progress on the ground?" Fu Wang the Intelligence Chief asked the local contact who had just arrived.

"Go on," said Wu Chin.

"We've successfully penetrated their network but it will take some time to figure out which node to compromise. The idea is to leave no digital trail and to maintain minimum footprint." Fu Wang explained in detail.

"How much time are we talking about here, to make it work, Fu? You must be aware that time is limited on this project," inquired Wu Chin.

"The intelligence we have indicates that this new weapon system of theirs has something to do with the new generation Geo-stationary satellite they launched recently," explained Jinn Wu "so we must focus on the internal divisions working on robotic system automation or military weapons ignoring all the other departments."

"Apart from that, we have another problem here," Fu Wang intervened. "We know that this new project is related to satellites but to what end? Is it a space based weapon, a new spying system or a navigational system for their weapons?"

"We must remember the information came through naval intelligence so it must be assumed that, whatever it is, it's related to the USA navy and its navigational system. So far the Americans don't have any space based weapon," the Intelligence Chief added.

"Well, gentlemen, discussion is futile at this point in time. Whatever it is will be revealed once we breach their servers. So, Fu, I'm going to repeat the question, how much time is it going to take you to penetrate into that network?" asked Wu Chin.

"A day or maybe even just a few hours from now," Fu Wang replied confidently.

"Very well, then I guess we're making some promising progress here," Wu Chin replied.

"Yes Wu, we are. As I said earlier, we're already in their network and scanning it now for firewalls and hardened servers," Fu Wang explained.

"Protocol demands you submit a complete report of your operation, Fu, with the specifics of your local contacts involved in the plan and details of how exactly you got into that network," Jinn Wu suddenly said. Everyone was aware of why Fu Wang had been asked to submit the particulars of the individual involved.

"Of course, Jinn. For now, I can tell you that we've been able to hack into the system using one of their guys in the finance division and I'll ensure that we'll complete with the minimum number of people involved."

"How many local people are involved so far?" Jinn Wu asked.

"One girl and another man on the inside," Fu replied.

Fu Wang lit a cigarette. Too many moving parts, he thought quietly. He was satisfied with the current progress but not so happy about the prospects of their current plan being successful. It was he who had reported to the Communist party leadership back in Beijing about this top secret USA Navy military project. He had been tasked to gather intelligence about the new system and proposed a line of action. If this was something significant and of national security, as his intelligence indicated, then this American project was going to challenge the build-up of the Chinese Navy in the South China Sea. China, in the last couple of decades, had closed the technological gap between themselves and the USA and was now busy overcoming the numerical superiority by building new surface and subsurface vessels.

“So, I think this concludes our business here,” he said putting his thoughts aside.

“I hope that we’ll hear some good news in next few hours from Fu Wang,” Wu Chin said, standing up. The others followed him and they left the warehouse.

***

Ajay Mohan, the charismatic CEO of Waverley Davis Incorporated, a multinational technology firm of global repute, was a celebrity in the technical world. An Indian by birth, he had emigrated to the USA three decades ago when he was a university student. His father was a successful trader whose import and export business was well established in India. It was he who had encouraged Ajay to pursue goals in his life. He had been sent to the USA for higher education when he showed no interest in the family business and had expressed his desire to go to America to make his own way in the world. Since his childhood he had been lucky in the sense that he met the right people at the right time who guided him just when he needed to be mentored.

His good luck continued after his arrival in the USA. His teachers and even his friends there had a big influence on his life, being sources of inspiration. His interaction with such people had shaped his subconscious. Throughout his life, he had unknowingly been taught about the Law of Attraction. He had only just recently realized this fact and now he wanted to transfer this knowledge to his son who he hoped would be his successor.

Ajay was different from others because his father had made him understand the importance of implementing learned knowledge into his practical life. New inventions, new technologies and new approaches had always been a great attraction for Ajay. Whenever he came across anything new, he would draw inspiration from it, making it part of his life. This habit of his had paid great dividends in later years.

"Remember, Ajay, internalizing any idea is as important as the idea itself," he still vividly remembered the advice of his father which had helped him greatly as an innovator of technology. It was his teacher, Professor Roberts, who had unlocked yet more secrets by making him understand that any desire for a change in our personality triggers a resistance from within. He had taught him that the human mind always wants to remain in a comfort zone. Our desire to bring about any change drags our mind outside that comfort zone and challenges the inner status quo. This is known as the Law of Attraction which defines our personality. Even years after completing his university degree, Ajay never stopped meeting up with his teacher in the hope of learning something new from him right up until the death of Professor Roberts a few years ago.

Ajay had married a Christian girl, Martha, who had been a classmate but, unlike Ajay, had a passion for art and fashion. When Ajay joined Waverley Davis Inc., a medium-sized enterprise providing solutions in industrial automation and communication technologies, Martha opened her own fashion house. Despite their different talents and occupations, both of them were alike. Both had similar temperaments and tastes.

It was Martha who had made Ajay understand the most valuable lesson in life when he faced a career crisis at Waverley Davis Inc. In his mind, he could still picture those turbulent times when he had struggled with proposing new ideas to his firm. All his ideas were rejected on a financial basis because the company management was unable to see any market value in his proposals. Somehow, he seemed unable to convince the management about the long term financial viability arising from the application of his ideas. He became very troubled and considered leaving his job. Martha helped him in a way he could never forget. It was she who told him he must stop thinking about changing his ideas and never stop pushing himself in search of something new.

"Dear, I think you need to change yourself," she had said and he would not forget this conversation which was to change him forever.

"What do you mean Martha? Don't you think I'm giving one hundred per cent when I'm working on these new ideas?" he asked her, puzzled.

"You're giving more than one hundred per cent and that's the problem," she replied.

"How come?" he asked, astonished by her response.

"I believe there's nothing wrong with your ideas but because you're concentrating too much on the technical aspects, you're ignoring the value of a good presentation strategy," she explained which set Ajay thinking.

"There's something to be changed and that change is required within you my love," Martha continued.

"Stop working on new ideas. Instead, why not try to change your approach by presenting the ideas you've already had in a different way. Make your firm realize that, in order to grow, they need to become the forerunners of change in market trends by implementing your ideas," she added. The solution had always been there but Ajay had been unable to see it.

"How can I change my presentation?" he asked.

"Let's get out of the city for couple of days and go somewhere else where you'll be able to connect with yourself and be think some more about it." Once again, she had immediately presented a solution.

Ajay had accepted her advice and they spent a weekend in Toronto and there Ajay finally realized what was wrong with his presentation strategy. He recalled that during meetings and presentations he would present only the technical aspects of the idea whilst the marketing aspects were usually presented by his immediate senior, Frank. Frank presented numbers and data sheets providing the management with the chance to raise various objections about the projected growth patterns. Ajay realized that neither he nor Frank had actually ever tried to tell their bosses about the future potential of their ideas and how they could influence market trends. They had never presented themselves as technology trend setters, merely followers of whatever trends had already been established in the market by others, including their competitors.

By the next meeting, Ajay had reworked his presentation. He avoided any technical or financial detail at this meeting and focused only on what his idea was and how it could change strategic decision making in large firms and financial institutions. His presentation was good enough to convince the then founder and CEO of Waverley Davis Inc. David Mackinder, who also told Ajay that he had presented his idea like a true leader of technology.

Hearing these remarks, all Ajay was able to think about later was what a valuable person Martha was in his life and how much he loved her. His ideas did indeed turn the technological tables and Waverley Davis began to emerge as a prominent player in the US technical market expanding its portfolio into other domains such as biotech and space sciences as well. He had been pushed to the edge of despair when his ideas were rejected time after time and he had almost made the decision to leave Waverley Davis until Martha led him to the discovery of something new in himself. Now he had the resolve to let nothing stand in the way of achieving his dreams. He had unknowingly completed all the stages of the Law of Attraction. Ajay and Martha felt their American dream was complete when their son, Jacob, was born three short years after their marriage. They considered many names for their son but settled on Jacob, a name which had been passed down through many generations in his mother's family.

Years passed by. Jacob turned out to be a bright student at school. He received a scholarship for a degree at MIT where he excelled, achieving a double major in emerging sciences and network security two years later. Ajay was proud of his son and, in Jacob, he could see his successor.

Then everything changed dramatically when the two men experienced the most tragic loss in their lives. Martha was killed in a road accident in Paris where she was working at a fashion exhibition.

Nothing was the same for Ajay after her death.

Memories of all the years spent with Martha gradually became too overwhelming for him. Now he wanted to leave, to find some solitude, at least for a few months but, with the current situation at work, all he could afford was a few hours off.

Jacob had joined Waverley Davis. The only reason for this was for the experience but now he had informed his father about his future plans. Ajay's reaction was natural.

"Are you out of your mind?" Ajay was confounded by his son's decision.

"No Dad, I'm your son but I'm also Mum's son as well that's all," Jacob had replied calmly.

"Meaning?" asked Ajay

"Tell me Dad, why did you reject your father's request to take care of his business when you were younger?" Jacob threw the ball back into Ajay's court. Suddenly, Ajay understood the meaning of Jacob's earlier reply.

"Dad, I believe that I too deserve a chance in life to be myself without using my father's name and the reputation of his firm," Jacob candidly explained his position.

"Yes, you do and best of luck, Son." Even Ajay had no clue why he gave that reply.

Over recent months, Ajay had many times imagined his son continuing to work in his business but this conversation between the two of them had left Ajay wondering if that would ever be a reality.

There was another matter which was proving to be a bone of contention between father and son. Ajay wanted to make his son understand the law of attraction so that he would achieve success in his life. This desire was even greater than seeing Jacob eventually become the head of Waverley Davis. Jacob, on the other hand, had always found it difficult to reconcile the ideas of universal laws and the connection between humans and unseen forces in the achievement of successful life.

"No Dad, I'm not interested in going to any seminar of this type." Jacob rejected the idea of going to a conference entitled "Spiritual Laws of the Cosmos" which was being organized by some Indian-American.

"The universe is governed by astrophysical laws, Dad. I cannot believe that I am hearing all this from a person who has spent his entire life following those principles." Once again Jacob's argument had a strong logical grounding, not easily contradicted. At least that was what Jacob had believed at that moment.

"And what do those astrophysical laws tell you about the people around you?" Ajay had an equally appropriate response.

Jacob searched for an answer but there was none forthcoming. He realized that it was time to surrender.

"For success, we must respect all the laws in the universe and, believe you me when I say this, there is much more in the vast expanse of cosmos than we can define with astrophysical laws. Just a minute ago, you came to realise that there are things which you need to learn." Ajay continued, making Jacob feel more uncomfortable within. The more he thought about an answer, the emptier he felt himself to be inside.

"I think I might give it a try, maybe there is something new to learn." His conscience had told him after failing to provide him with any suitable answer to Ajay's argument. "But there won't be anything scientific to learn in this workshop." Resistance kicked in from within. "Anyway, I'll go." Finally a decision was made.

After this discussion, with Jacob having decided to attend the workshop, on his way to the venue, he constantly thought about his own ideas of the new operating system he had been working on since last year. He wanted to introduce a mobile OS capable of learning the likes and dislikes of its users which could configure and personalize itself according to the trends of its user. The most innovative aspect of his idea was the ability of this OS to study the emerging security risks and make changes in its kernel.

He took a seat on the back row at the conference and found nothing much to look at there. Soon a presenter appeared and introduced the topic of the workshop. Jacob considered almost all of the ideas presented throughout the workshop to be empty claims with no scientific basis. The presenter promoted the idea of defining a purpose in life without worrying about the means and ways to achieve that purpose.

"All you need to understand is where you want to go. Don't think too much about how you'll get there. Leave that to a power greater than yourself." One of the workshop participants was on the podium. "Leaving the strategy to some higher power, how is that possible?" Jacob had thought, "and isn't this in direct contradiction of one of the earlier speakers who was of the opinion that we are the most important component in the greater scheme of things in the cosmos and it's our own thoughts which define our reality. How can they both be right the same time?" Resistance within had become palpable now. He walked out of the workshop. A few days later, he tried another seminar on a similar topic and had not forgotten to tell Ajay about his visit to this second seminar although he found it to be as equally boring as the first.

Jacob had not realized at that time that he was not attending these workshops and seminars to learn anything but merely to satisfy his father. This had been his mission since his school days, not to disappoint his father. He had not gained any benefit by attending the workshop and seminar as he had not learnt anything new. While sitting in the seminars he would constantly be thinking about his idea of building a self-learning secure operating system.

Jacob had idealized his parents as the perfect couple, made for each other. The bond of love between the two had proved to be the biggest inspiration in his life. He imagined a life partner for himself just like his mother had been to his father but he was not lucky like Ajay.

Jacob had grown up in the post-modern era where many of his friends and even some of his teachers had told him that morality was an excuse of the weak and to attain success in life one must be capable of being ruthless. This was contrary to everything he had seen at home and what his parents had taught him. Most of the time he would think his parents' guidance was right but, under certain other circumstances, he would consider his teachers and classmates to be correct. This had sown a seed of uncertainty in his subconscious which he was totally unaware of. Now, when he had started to attend these seminars, that seed of conflict within his personality was growing into a tree. This made him doubtful as to whether he would ever find a life partner like the one he imagined.

Elsewhere, Ajay was worried about his son as well as his business. He was not worried about Jacob's success in life, he knew that his son was fully capable of turning his dreams into a reality just like Ajay had done in his life. It was his well-considered opinion that, without learning certain secrets of life, his son would find it very difficult to cope with the challenges that lay ahead. Ajay was not wrong in his assessment but he did not realize that he was trying to push his son too soon towards things which he was not yet ready to learn.

Chapter Two

What you think you become, What you feel you attract,
What you imagine you create.

Buddha

Today, Waverley Davis is one of the leading technology firms in the world. It has a business portfolio encompassing many hi-tech domains - IT, Biotech, Robotics, Artificial Intelligence (AI), Space Sciences and Pharmaceuticals. Each domain is headed by an expert in each specialized field. Ajay had realized that, in order to stay relevant in the market, Waverley Davis would have to grow. Apart from becoming more creative in existing portfolios, the company needed to venture into new domains as well in order to become a pioneer and trendsetter in the technological market.

Since its inception, Waverley Davis had worked with US military forces but not as a main contractor. Today, Waverley Davis was the leading partner in many US military related projects particularly in satellite engineering, navigational system and robotics. But there was a flipside to this achievement. After accepting military contracts, the firm found itself drawn into high intensity, global cyber warfare between China, Russia and the USA. Many freelance hacker groups had also been involved in this war and they would usually act like guns for hire. Freelance hacker groups were a big attraction for foreign governments and espionage agencies as they would provide plausible scapegoats in case any operation went awry.

Victor McCrery was a network architecture and internet security expert. He headed the Waverley Davis cyber security wing and reported directly to the CEO. He had designed the Waverley Davis network which had multi-layered security systems developed for special applications implemented through various firewalls, Demilitarized Zones (DMZs) and Virtual Private Networks (VPNs). More sensitive network nodes were completely isolated where only selected people had access. Data backups were heavily encrypted. Very secure and a hard network to hack into; at least this is was what the Waverley Davis security team in the IT department believed before the first wave of highly sophisticated cyber-attacks hit their network.

The entire IT department was under siege after Victor had discovered that hackers had tried to penetrate the perimeter firewalls. Lock down of the department was one of the Standard Operating Procedures (SOPs). Victor was getting updates from his team every few minutes. Log files of various network firewalls and intrusion detection systems were appearing on his screen.

"What's the status of physical security?" Victor asked tersely.

"There's been no physical breach. All premises are secure," Farrell, his assistant, replied with his fingers skipping quickly across his keyboard.

"Perimeter firewalls were attacked but there's nothing in these logs. If they'd succeeded, our web gateways would have been exposed." Victor was still busy checking the network traffic patterns.

"Was it DDOS?" he wondered out loud.

"Distributed Denial of Service?" Farrell queried and continued "The type of DDOS attack where multiple compromised systems are often infected? That means both the end targeted system and all systems can be maliciously used and controlled by the hacker in the distributed attack."

"No, I've dealt with those types of attacks. This one is too sophisticated to be a DDOS attack." Victor was convinced that this was no ordinary attempt on their network which was pretty self-sufficient in thwarting ordinary attacks. "They didn't want to choke the network, they were trying to breach it. Question is, to what end?" Victor expressed his concerns.

"As far as we know, the traffic packets responsible for this attempt were initiated from Asian and European networks but there were definitely US based hackers involved as well," Farrell informed Victor about the origin of attack. He was still running his network security suite to generate more analysis reports.

"That's not important. Most probably they were all using VPN."

"Well, our system pushed them out of our network that's all that matters in the end," Farrell announced with satisfaction.

"How do we know that they're not going to try it again?" asked Victor grimly.

"We don't. But by now they should have a pretty good idea about our network security mechanisms," said Farrell, still believing in victory.

"They'll come with new malware next time, one with an even nastier payload," Victor expressed his concerns. He knew that hackers liked to penetrate hardened networks. This was characteristic of them. Now the Waverley Davis network was in their crosshair.

"Boss, I think we're just overthinking today's events. Cyber-attacks are an undeniable reality of the 21st century. The CIA, FBI and Office of Personnel Management all got attacked and hacked. Basically, it depends on how strong your network is to prevent a complete hack. To me, some nerdy minds with crazy ideas have tried their luck by breaking into one of the largest corporate networks in the world," Farrell argued.

"If you still think they're going to come with something new and nastier, then they're not the only ones who can learn from their mistakes. We'll harden our defences even more by patching any vulnerability in the network," Farrell continued.

"Farrell, I want you to run a heuristic analysis of all network traffic in the past three days. There must be some clue there," Victor instructed. "I need those reports as soon as possible. I want to patch the network to make the intrusion prevention system more pro-active," he added. Farrell nodded to Victor although he was still convinced that Victor was overreacting to the situation.

"I'm going to farm to check the status of the isolated nodes," Victor said standing up. They used the word 'farm' for the server farm that was located in the lower basement of the Waverley Davis building.

Two years ago, Waverley Davis had won the contract for a top secret classified project for the US Navy. The project was of strategic importance because it was about to play a key role in a new war doctrine of the US Navy in strategic hotspots around the globe. The project aimed to implement the rapid deployment and early assessment of the battlefield. Since the beginning of the project, the Waverley Davis communication and IT division had been in the process of developing specialized intelligent algorithms. The US military was going to use the final software application on its next generation spy satellites and destroyers. The distributed systems were to help the US Navy in identifying friendly and hostile ships in open oceans instantly cutting down the critical time in which military ships could track and identify enemy ships after painting them with various kinds of radars. A second goal of the system was to present all the data graphically in Pentagon real time so that operational decision making could be effected as quickly as possible.

The Chinese, Russians, Israelis and British were all interested in building a similar system. A system like this was going to give the USA and its allies a clear advantage over competitors. The Pentagon had considered this project a fine deterrent against the growing number of maritime assets owned by the Chinese and Russian Navies at a juncture of history where the US Navy was faced with budgetary cuts.

***

Meanwhile, Ping May the overall Chinese Intelligence Chief who returned to China, had carefully considered most of the various possible scenarios which could emerge after the attack. He wanted to have a contingency plan in place for every development. He was particularly concerned about a possible trail he may have left, leading to the Americans investigating this all the way back to Beijing. He was in his office along with a taller younger man. Unlike Ping May, the young man wore civilian clothes but his distinctive body shape and overall demeanor indicated an obvious background in military training. They were waiting there for a further guest who was shortly to arrive from the United States.

He pulled out his cigarette lighter and puffed on another cigarette, blowing a mottled ring of smoke and, after a slight pause, sighed. Just then his assistant informed him of the arrival of his guest. He welcomed his guest with enthusiasm when he realized it was Jinn Wu. Pleasantries were exchanged and now Jinn Wu was waiting for Ping May to speak.

There was a long silent pause then, in a quiet voice, Ping May asked "Do you have any update on our cyber plan?" He waited before Jinn Wu answered, "Yes, we're making some progress, the resistance from their system is far greater than we and our team anticipated but our grid has tried to trace their network and they're pretty confident that they'll get into it soon."

"Hmm… I see but what have you thought about the aftermath?" Ping May enquired.

"We'll have to deal with that later, this project is far too well established to worry about any afterthoughts," he replied calmly.

After a moment, Ping May said, "No Jinn Wu, that's where you're wrong, we do have to have contingencies in place for every possible outcome. Beijing is concerned about this secretive project and no one in the party would like any possible lead tracing these attacks to China. We're not doing it for the sake of money or any other short term gain. We want our sea borders and territory secure so that no intruder from the other side of the Pacific Rim can violate our space. It's about achieving peace by maintaining the status quo which right now favours the Chinese defense systems in the region. This is how important this is as a strategic operation."

Perplexed, Jinn Wu asked, "So what do you propose?"

Ping May considered the question and then replied "I think we must not underestimate the Americans' superior technical advantage in cyber technology. By now, their cyber command will be investigating these attacks so prepare yourself along with Fu Wang and his team and, whatever happens, make no contact especially via the American communication networks. Most of all, try to maintain minimum contact with him as well," Ping concluded.

"We're already careful in this regard. We use our normal security grid protocol but we'll take extra care. Most important of all, you must keep our ambassador updated without meeting Fu Wang regularly."

"Ok, but I'm going to send Lee with you." Ping pointed towards the third guy in the room who, until now, had stood silently listening intently to their conversation. He continued, "Lee is one of my top agents and has completed many assignments overseas involving stealth operations, information recovery, espionage and secret program egress, recovering secretive communication and we've also used him for human target assassinations."

"He'll help us in communicating with Fu Wang secretly, I guess," Jinn Wu conceded.

"If instructed, he'll do all of the things in his brief or anything else expected of him," Ping boasted with a smirk on his face.

"So that does include assassinations?" with a look of confusion, Jinn Wu had finally figured out that Lee was in fact Ping's hit-man.

Still perplexed he continued, "But we didn't discuss any assassination during our meeting." Looking bewildered, he went on, "Do you realize just how big a problem you have here? And an even bigger diplomatic crisis for China if he gets caught there," he said panicking.

Ping thought about his answer then replied, "He's working as a grid operative who will operate invisibly as far as you're concerned. That's one of the reasons for me making you meet him. Most of his work will be carried out in the United States, if he gets caught in the US, we, of course, will never acknowledge him or even accept him as a Chinese national. He already knows the operational protocol in diplomacy espionage so he's trained to do only what he has to do in that particular scenario. Let us all hope that it will not come to that."

Things were making some sense at last for Jinn Wu but he still had questions. "Who will he assassinate there?" he asked cautiously.

"Well who do you expect? Obviously," he explained, "Fu Wang, his team and anyone else working with them. This is where he'll be undertaking his mission and, in espionage terms, working as a spook. He'll take care of all the equipment including the operatives involved. Clearing the grid afterwards even if they do not deliver."

"That is why," Ping concluded, "we cannot leave any loose ends or unfinished business. Their elimination would turn this scenario into a murder investigation not a cyber-crime investigation."

Ping explained the cover story he had in mind. The Chinese Embassy would create a false identity for Lee in case he got caught. He proceeded to show that, that according to these documents, Lee was a North Korean business man undertaking overseas work on a placement to the US. He then handed a false passport and other papers including a work visa in a brown envelope to Jinn Wu. This practice was standard protocol on such a mission.

Their meeting concluded. The next day, Jinn Wu left for the USA and, unbeknown to him, Lee was already there in New York on holiday as a Korean tourist taking a short holiday before he began work.

***

Farrell was gazing at the heuristic analysis report of the most recent cyber-attack and, whilst studying it, a confused look developed on his face. This was only a few hours after he and Victor had had the conversation about the nature of hackers. "Does it contain anything serious?" Victor asked Farrell as he entered the room.

"Not sure. But it seems something's not quite right with this data analysis," he replied still gazing at the reports.

"Let me have a look." Victor walked over to him spreading out his hand and, using a highlighter to mark a set of figures with a bright yellow ring, Farrell handed over those pages that he had already checked. Victor started to check the results too and after few minutes he also had a worried look on his face.

Scowling at the figures, he commented, "How someone out there could have presented guess work like this about our internal internet provider schemes is a complete mystery to me."

Victor read for a few minutes then continued, "Certainly, someone who has a good understanding of our internal network's location addressing scheme is not just a 'nerdy mind with some crazy idea', my man of volar." Victor's reply left Farrell speechless. He was fully aware why Victor had used the literal meaning of his name.

"So what do we do now boss?" Farrell asked.

"We'll have to take a look into the payload of these traffic packets apart from tracing their origin." Victor was thoughtful. "If the attack is sophisticated, it seems that they are not after something specific but they want to stay in the network undetected for a longer period of time. Had they intended just to bypass firewalls they would have adopted bypassing techniques but they didn't even try any of those. The malware encapsulated in these packets seems very sophisticated. We'll have to examine that in order to understand their end game."

Victor continued to decipher various dynamics of the attack. "So we'll have to put that payload in a sandbox to study it. If someone has gone to these lengths, he's not attacking us just to cripple us. He certainly wants to take over the network. This is definitely not their last attempt," he concluded.

"We can only sniff a few packets to put in a sandbox for testing now before the next attack. We don't know when that will be. What are we are going to do until then?" Farrell asked.

“We’ll find the rat inside this organization who provided the opportunity to these hackers by leaking the IP scheme of our internal network,” Victor said with a determined look on his face.

***

“How was your session at the last seminar?” Ajay asked Jacob about his experience at his latest outing. They were having dinner together several days later and, although Jacob was not yet ready for this sort of conversation, not answering his father’s question was also not an option.

“It was interesting, Dad, but not good enough for my liking. I’ve got more questions than I had before I went there” Jacob said after some hesitation. This came as no surprise to Ajay but he was happy that now at least his son was discussing this topic with him. Until recently, Ajay could not have had this conversation with him because Jacob would become annoyed about the subject.

“What questions do you have on your mind, Son?” Ajay asked, hoping that he would be able to help to clear Jacob’s thoughts.

“Well Dad, I’m not sure what the purpose is of a higher power in the cosmos if human will is the most critical element capable of changing and reshaping the reality?” Jacob asked calmly. Ajay had not expected this particular question but was well aware that in order to maintain his son's interest in the conversation he would have to come up with a satisfactory answer. He needed some time to think so he chose to ask a counter question.

"Did you ask this question in the seminar?"

"No Dad. Neil called and I had to leave just before the usual Q & A session at the end," Jacob lied. He had left the seminar midway and Neil had not called him that day at all. He had figured out that his father was trying to avoid his question. He wanted to keep Ajay on the topic he had introduced.

"Ok. Let's talk about human will first," Ajay started. "What do the latest quantum physics experiments tell us about the connection between reality and human observation? They tell us that…"

"That reality doesn't exist if you're not looking at it," Jacob intervened. He had also read about the experiments carried out by a lab in Australia.

"Exactly!" Ajay's voice got louder. "So what does that tell you about the impact of human observation and the nature of reality?" he asked.

"These experiments you're talking about were conducted in a controlled environment to study certain laws of quantum physics. But, still, I'm not sure if we can declare the nature of reality as illusionary based on these findings," Jacob argued.

"I want you to concentrate on the role of human observation here more than anything else. And do you have any proof that contradicts these findings?" Ajay asked and Jacob knew that he had a very tight space in which to maneuver now. Scientifically, he could not disprove the experiments which had revealed that reality has a direct link to human observation. Now he wanted to change the topic. It was easy for him to reject the spirituality hiding behind the laws of physics but from the same standpoint, it was impossible for him to deny quantum physics.

"And, as for our reality, what we believe determines what we make true," Ajay told Jacob.

"This is where I always lose you, Dad," Jacob protested. "Why does belief always comes into a discussion about making rational choices?" he questioned with more than a little agitation in his tone.

"Because all our reality is built upon our perceptions. In fact, it's our thoughts that create our reality which is why we are defined by what we look for and we look for what we need in our lives," Ajay replied in a calm manner. "Ancient philosophers spoke of this two thousand years ago. Try to understand, it's not something we humans have discovered recently. The Roman philosopher Marcus Aurelius, a Roman Gladiator and philosopher, said, "That our light is what our thoughts make of it."

He continued, “Just look at this particular dichotomy. It’s your belief wrongly, that, it’s our conscious mind that makes our decisions and is the focal instrument within the human that enables us to make rational choices. This is in fact inaccurate; although our conscious mind helps, it’s not the engine of life.”

Jacob looked perplexed and had a growing feeling that his Dad was talking absolute rubbish. In fact, he had never heard such nonsense.

Ajay tried again, softening his tack somewhat. “What you need to understand, Jacob, is that there is immense power in your subconscious mind.” He explained that you need to realize that fact, concentrate on the creative side of your subconscious and that, when you understood that dichotomy, you could in fact shape reality.

This lecture was a little on the heavy side for Jacob and was delivered as if he was in a philosophy class. He still thought this was all rubbish saying “Dad, please, can we have this conversation at some other time. I’m tired of this fantasy of yours which always makes me wonder how a pragmatic individual like you can say things like this!” Jacob shouted.

After dinner was eaten, they sat, barely exchanging a single word, almost in complete silence and then each left for their respective rooms shortly afterwards. Jacob put the conversation out of his mind as he always did. Ajay was deeply troubled as, once again, he was saddened by the fact that he could not make his son understand what he wanted him to grasp.

***

The next day, Victor and his team were once again made busy with another cyber-attack by the hackers. This time Victor had prepared for it and had a plan ready. He had configured the network in such a way that all the incoming network data packets were waiting to be sorted, like huge fishing nets full of fish with some rogue ones as well. The data packets could be captured this time in a few isolated servers for the Waverly Davis technicians to study later on.

In network jargon, he had created a honeypot. He had secretly put software in place which put them safely in a demilitarized zone on the network thereby ensuring that the internal networks remained secure. His plan worked but only for a few minutes. Suddenly the attack changed tactics where the inward flow of traffic into the honeypot simply vanished, just as had happened during the previous attack. However, this time he captured some encrypted packet payloads from the outside source meaning he could ascertain the actual payload data identity attached with these packets.

Victor typed on the server dashboard keypad at breakneck speed to stay up with this encryption thinking, "Here's something I've never seen before." His command prompts sent the server software directly into the isolated DMZ area command mode. Enter, enter, enter quickly he pressed on the keyboard and his command created new lines on the screen. He was now connected to the isolated network which they had placed in DMZ in order to gather cyber-attack forensics.

"This is one very clever virus attack," he snorted. "This is more sophisticated than the average malware or viruses usually are," he explained. "This means that they tried to send a portion of an encrypted file on an outbound interface. Normally you need to have disabled interfaces and then opened many logical ports. However, with this virus and malware, both are designed to do specific tasks and only work if their target network has any vulnerability which can be exploited. Difference is, this is much more subtle. It can create its own vulnerabilities."

"Explained simply," he continued, "a user's web browser is hijacked by a drive-by download and redirected to an exploit kit which probes the user's computer and applications for vulnerabilities. Once vulnerability is found, a malicious payload is downloaded onto the victim's computer (infection). Finally, the malware (in this case also called ransom ware) attempts to extort money from the victim or, in our case, destroy our product or worse disable it. With that in mind I'm wondering if the payload had actually reprogrammed itself after I made the changes to the network security.

More worrying for me, is how someone could have changed it afterwards and how come in such a short span of time? This must therefore be either an internal plant or, because of the clever complexity, an outside attempt to hack us." Victor was concerned in any event after watching the sophistication of this payload. Worse still, that it could be an inside job.

If it is the latter, he thought, then we'll have to find whoever is responsible inside our company network. If they can design something like this, with this payload, I'm certain they can mask their outside attack within our network as well. The more important questions are the reasons behind the attack on our server and what they are trying to achieve here.

Victor continued to investigate, reading data and considering the breach. The more he thought about it, if his suspicions were right, then they had always been a step ahead of us in this game. The more he thought about it, the more he became convinced that someone from inside Waverley Davis was responsible. In any event, it pointed to a very skillful individual who was conspiring against the firm.

"This is a similar attack to a hi-tech industrial espionage operation," Victor commented.

Regardless of the question of the final agenda, he added that the main concern was the need to focus on the central problem which was to keep the network secure without spreading any panic.

“I think that we need to bring it to the urgent attention of Ajay,” Farrell ventured.

“No, before we do that, first we need to understand the threat,” Victor replied.

As soon as the words left Victor’s lips, he was interrupted by Farrell shouting, “You must see this!” Victor quickly looked at the screen to where Farrell was pointing and was astonished to see their captured data had somehow been deleted and now there was no trace of it at all. They had seen it just moments before.

“Someone just deleted the captured data,” he said. “And amazingly it looks like all the opened ports have been closed,” Farrell added with a confused look on his face.

“We’re not the only one accessing that isolated node; someone else is also in there live online now,” he said.

“Yes and whoever is doing this, they’re actually removing the malware and restoring the server to its previous state.” Victor was also bewildered how this could get past their firewall and complicated grid defense system, most of which he had designed, let alone be a live cyber-attack.

"I'm trying to trace the Internet Protocol to identify this hacker," Farrell muttered.

In an instant, the session was terminated by them. Just as quickly, they were gone.

"Wait, none of this makes any sense," said Victor "First someone attacked us, got into our honeypot and then someone else came in to help to remove all the traces. What is happening or, more importantly, what does this make the second intruder?" Victor mused. He now had had more questions than answers.

"We need more time to get to the bottom of this," Farrell said, stating the obvious.

"Yes and as quickly as possible. We can't keep this away from Ajay's office for too long now. We need to break it to him before someone else does," Victor added in desperation.

Within ninety minutes, another attack began. Only this time, the hackers were a lot more prepared for what they expected by way of defense. They had by-passed the perimeter firewall security in a mega-second, trying to get into the internal network inside the isolated area DMZ which was set aside for isolated node capture. In computer security terms, a DMZ or demilitarized zone (sometimes referred to as a perimeter network) was normally well-protected by firewall security. In this attempt however, the firewall was by-passed in seconds and immediate internal access was achieved.

Victor knew that the Protocol in his operating system definitely used DHCP on this network server. The Dynamic Host Configuration Protocol (DHCP) is a standard network protocol. That meant servers like DHCP and DNS were all located on the other side of this firewall with access to control servers and if storage servers were accessed then they would be massively compromised. If there was any breach of the usual network firewall, a DNS server area on his mainframe was the target attacking web host software registered to intercept the collective Domain Name System. He knew that this attack specifically targeted his DNS server. That meant if extreme firewall violation had occurred then it was it had reached the destination they had intended.

More worryingly, he had to consider a breach in the internal firewall could mean possible access to his web and mail servers. This was a potential doomsday scenario for the Waverley Davis network. Something a military computer security firm like this could never afford.

These hackers were too audacious, not giving enough time for Victor to properly analyze payload and attack patterns. To make it worse, for every attack they kept changing, using different techniques. This meant the cyber security team of Waverley Davis had to try to guess the hackers' next move. Victor also decided to increase the resources dedicated to the analysis of the job. He knew in order to keep the network secure he would have to put more positive security hardware in place urgently. This meant he had no choice but to tell the CEO about their current predicament.

But for now, they had an attack to fend off as they were under attack for the third time that day. Meanwhile, Farrell, along with everybody in his team, was really nervous. Thankfully for Waverley Davis, Farrell had a better tolerance level for panic and, on the outside at least, he appeared calmer than the others. He was a little like a swan though as, right to the pit of his stomach, he was worried. He visualized the media in a post attack scenario where the Waverley Davis name would no doubt appear in the leading newspapers and on the major TV channels. Imagine a more negative impact of adverse media coverage than telling the world about flaws in its own cyber security.

Then another scenario entered his head where he saw himself having to resign and leave Waverley Davis altogether, shuffling out of the building, head down and hung in shame. He took a deep breath and changed the image in his mind, thus forcing his subconscious mind to imagine another scene. In this version of events, the attack had just been diverted by some unseen force.

‘Just imagine,’ he said to himself, ‘that I’m the one de-cyphering these nasty viruses and that all threats have been mitigated.’ This technique had been introduced to the entire workforce by Ajay, the CEO, who had taught it to many of his workers in order to change their mindset. It was called the Law of Attraction.

He had told them whenever their subconscious mind conjured up something disturbing about their future, they should clearly imagine their goals without thinking too much about the means and ways of achieving them. Help will come from unexpected sources he had told them. Most of them, however, ridiculed the logic of this in a real world situation. Farrell thankfully was much more opened minded.

The computer attack continued with full force. “Look here, they’re inside our network.” Farrell shouted, back in the room from his world of imagination and now looking at the screens in front of him. He wanted to know which server the hackers would try to break into now after bypassing the second firewall.

Amazingly, nothing happened even after ten minutes of intrusion. They were looking at the logs for any update triggered by any activity. Thankfully nothing, when, just then, he noticed that they had someone inside the DNS gateway server. They were altering authentication certificates and they were being reconfigured.

Farrell informed Victor immediately, “The certificates are being reconfigured.”

“What do you mean reconfigured?” Victor asked.

“The certificates are being altered,” he replied.

Victor was furious because the hackers had breached the defenses of what he would consider to be a cyber-fortress. “What the hell?” he said in a flabbergasted tone. “They’re out now and it seems that only the one hacker was able to penetrate into our gateway which now has a new set of authentication certificates configured. I’m going to inspect these now but I can tell you that this mysterious hacker was the same one we encountered earlier today in our honeypot server.”

He continued, “Whoever this hacker is, he is not only very familiar with our network but also knows a way around this malicious payload. He also continues to attack us from various origins. This means that we have something on our network that information is required by many destinations from anywhere on the planet. Perhaps more than one source at the same time and our network has been rendered into a cyber-battlefield.”

Victor made the observation that, apart from themselves, at least two other parties were competing for control of this server. He could not explain how he had imagined a very similar scenario only a few minutes earlier and was equally amazed by the fact that what he had visualized had become reality so quickly. This remained a mystery even though he was aware of the Law of Attraction. 'The network on the server was secure for now at least,' he thought.

This was not the first time he had summoned help while under pressure without doing a thing about it yet help had come instantly purely by releasing the thought. Whenever he did this, the server responded and outside help came quickly. Now he was thinking about bringing the matter to Ajay's attention and asking him to help by advising him as to the best line of action. Suddenly, he had another picture in his mind where he and his boss Ajay were discussing this matter with two other people. They were all discussing a response strategy but Victor was not able to figure out who the other two people were in his vision. He was only able to see two figures, no more than faint silhouettes.

Chapter Three

"Religion is the opiate of the masses."

Karl Marx

"However, the opiate of today's masses are computers."

Len Marshall

He had completed the first phase of his task in the US. He had marked all his potential targets and, except for one, had succeeded in bugging them. Now he was able to hear every word that was spoken among his target group. Listen and report. He recalled his mission there once again. He was to take care of the situation as instructed in case anyone from this group became a potential threat to the plans of his benefactors.

Now he was tailing his primary target. He wanted to tag one remaining female member of the group. He had her picture but did not know her whereabouts. He continued tailing his target into a restaurant. He was in the disguise of an elderly man with glasses and a pencil mustache.

Lee took a seat three tables away from his target and ordered coffee. He could see the back of his target who was waiting for someone. Lee took his mobile out and initiated an app which showed an animation of a magnifying glass accompanying the text "Searching Target Device" below it. Soon his mobile was connected to another mobile device with its microphone turned on. He connected his mobile to his earphones and took a sip of coffee while staring at the back of his target. Soon a blonde girl appeared in the restaurant to meet his target. A smirk appeared on his face. He had his next target right in front of him.

***

"Why have you only just told me about these attacks today?" Ajay was clearly shocked after learning about the cyber-attacks on Waverley Davis.

Victor was at a meeting with Ajay, arranged immediately after Ajay had received Victor's email only a few minutes earlier. He continued, "You should have informed me right from the onset of the attacks." This, being a matter of major concern, had forced Ajay to cancel his diary of endless meetings for that day, just to urgently address this situation.

"Well, I had to assess the scale of the attacks and initially that was not clear," Victor said quietly. "As head of security, I made an assessment that these types of attacks from various hacking groups seeking access to our server are considered normal activity, so I didn't bother you with it," Victor replied defensively.

"Your email said that there was no data lost or theft from our server even though our firewalls were breached. How do you explain that?" Ajay asked.

"It appears, strangely enough, that there was someone in our network, there just to help us. It's a complete mystery and totally unfathomable," Victor replied. "Running analyses time and time again, my expert opinion is that our network was a target for more than one attack and it became a battlefield where one group tried to stop the other group, so both were acting at the same time. In short, we are victims of two or more groups of hackers who are vying for control more than anything else. It could be that that someone has found out about one of our military security strategic projects and wants to copy it," Victor said.

"I was told about that possibility but didn't take it seriously," Ajay said. "More importantly, what measures are we using to protect our network?"

"We've put various measures in place to increase the security of all network nodes in the research and development department of each division but so far we've no idea what they actually want," Victor replied.

"Can you expand upon your previous statement that you were told about this possibility, what does that mean?" Victor added.

"As you know, Victor, this is not the first military related project we have rolled out here at Waverley. This time, however, it's highly classified and of a much more secretive nature. That's all I can tell you because of the secrecy clauses in the contracts," Ajay concluded.

Victor understood the need for discretion and remarked, "That's all I needed to know right now." He understood the motives of these hackers. "I'll run various attack scenarios and mitigate the vulnerabilities to plug any loophole in the military division's network," he added.

"We need to keep a lid on this," Ajay continued. "Victor, who else is aware of this particular situation?"

"Within Waverley Davis, you are only one of eight people after myself, my assistant Farrell and five others working in my team," Victor informed him.

"Thank you and I would like to keep it that way if we can," Ajay added. "No one else must know about this. Please increase the security as you deem necessary and please make sure that nobody externally gets to know about this situation. We're not going to give the world's business media any ammunition to paint us in a negative light. Those media-tech savvy reader types do not usually understand technical issues and believe whatever they read or listen to in the media."

We must remember that even the reputations of large multinational companies like Sony and IBM received negative publicity after both were hacked. We, as an organization, cannot afford that sort of PR disaster." "I can understand that Ajay, you can rest assured no one will ever know anything," Victor said a little nervously. "To maintain secrecy and continue to deal with this matter covertly, don't even mention this business, not on the telephone anytime whether on or off office premises please. We'll discuss this on a need to know basis and, even then, only when the need arises." Victor thought that Ajay was behaving perhaps a little over cautiously and maybe a little too insecurely but understood the need for overzealous caution. On the other hand, Ajay's reaction was driven by the inherent fear of losing the trust of his clients and their confidence in his ability to provide unparalleled security, At least for the security of the customers of Waverley Davis, as investors in the military software business.

After all, Ajay had spent most of his working life making big strategic decisions in the business world and, as such, was well-aware of the rapid pace in which technology was reshaping our world.

His confidence in Victor and his team was not even shaken after the attacks.

Meanwhile, Victor was once again reflecting that this malware was different because it was not exploiting vulnerability in an existing case but creating its own weaknesses to gain access to the server. On the whole, it was impossible to spot, let alone stop.

Victor once again had disturbing visions of possible scenarios which his imagination was creating.

The question was what was his inner mind trying to tell him?

***

Ajay had left for home early after his meeting with Victor.

He awaited the arrival of the report regarding enhanced network security that he had instructed to come to his home address.

Luckily, when Ajay reached home, Jacob was already there. They both sat in the lounge where Jacob was watching a local baseball game, the New York Yankees versus the Baltimore Orioles.

Masahiro Tanaka hit a tremendous pitch as Ajay looked up but there was a very unnerving silence between them. "Home run," he quipped. Both kept watching the television screen for few minutes.

Their last encounter was playing on Jacob's his mind and he wanted to say sorry to Ajay but was struggling to find the right words. He glanced at his father's face and thought he looked tired and seemed thoughtful about something serious. "Dad, are you ok? You look really tired."

"I'm perfectly alright, thanks," replied Ajay.

He continued to gaze at the television screen but Jacob realized that although Ajay seemed to be concentrating on the baseball, his mind was actually elsewhere.

"I think maybe I should have some rest after all," Ajay said as he stood up.

Jacob was still thinking about the other day and their previous conversation. He wanted to say sorry for his behavior when his Dad had been answering his questions about having free will. He had thought about that day over and over again and now, when he had finally met up with his father again, he found him to be very tired. "Is it due to me? No, it can't be. He was happy when I saw him talking on the phone when I was leaving for the gym," he thought. "Then what's bothering him like this?" he wondered.

***

There was no attack during the next three days and Victor was happy. He had reconfigured and redesigned a few more network nodes and wanted to brief Ajay about it. He was in Ajay's office. "Good job Victor, I hope we're safe now," Ajay said after looking at the report regarding the new network security measures. "We can never say that with certainty in this day and age," Victor replied ruefully. "However, the network is now much stronger than it was before." After a brief pause he added, "I was thinking you should consider involving the FBI just in case."

"Victor, I've already told you about the options of doing that. Press releases, clarifications, retractions, colorful stories on social media and the internet about us. We simply can't afford all of that," Ajay said.

"Ajay, we need the FBI. Not as protection but to help us find the culprits. This could be a matter of national security. We can't take the law into our own hands," Victor argued.

"So, you're telling me that our own team is not capable of keeping our network secure?" Ajay asked.

"No, Ajay, that's not the case. We are more than capable of keeping the network secure but we can't apprehend the culprits, that's a task for the FBI. They can establish the origin of this attack," Victor said.

"We need to talk to someone inside the FBI cybercrime department who can be trusted with such information."

Victor knew exactly who to speak to.

***

Neil was Jacobs's closest friend and also worked in the Waverley Davis Finance Department. They had grown up together and, despite having similar preferences in many things, they both had their own passions which had led them to make different choices in their professional education once they had finished their mainstream schooling.

Jacob had opted to pursue his technical dream whilst Neil had attended a financial education institute. He had joined Waverley three years ago when Jacob was still in MIT. Over the years, many people had come and gone in both their lives but they had remained constants in each other's. Their friendship was known throughout the firm. Jacob enjoyed this permanent connection to the place and so became a regular visitor to Waverley.

That day he was there in Neil's office. Neil was surprised to see him there so early; he usually came in the afternoon. Jacob's surprise visit excited Neil because he wanted to share his big secret with his best friend.

"Nothing can resist a human will that will stake even its existence on its stated purpose," Neil read a Benjamin Disraeli's quote.

"Inspiring, isn't it? You know, nothing has inspired me more than that quote - to have a clearly defined purpose in life is important for the success of our will," Neil said with a smile.

"I don't know about that my friend but that's not why I'm here," Jacob said.

"Do you need some advice?" Neil asked, thinking that Jacob might be there to seek his opinion on some financial matter regarding his idea of setting up his own IT firm.

"It's about Dad. Do you think he's behaving in a strange manner? Does he seem worried to you lately?" Jacob inquired.

"What do you mean? He's the same as always, full of energy and positivity. I just saw him a few minutes ago" Neil replied but Jacob was standing quiet and still. "Sit here and tell me what's bothering you about him."

"He's not right, Neil. I've never seen him tired like this and he's been like it for the last three days." Jacob voice held concern. "Actually, sometimes I think he might be disturbed because of me," he added soberly. "Other times, it feels as if he's hiding something from me."

"Why do you think that?" Neil asked.

"We had an argument earlier this week at dinner when he tried to explain a few things about life to me and I didn't agree with him," Jacob said. Neil was still perplexed. He was well-aware of their disagreements on topics related to spirituality.

"What's happened Jacob, what did you do?" Neil asked.

"I shouted at him and the next day when he came home, he seemed tired and disturbed. Now I feel disappointed with myself," Jacob told him.

"Jacob, I've always been envious of you, that Ajay is your father, not because of his wealth or social standing but because of his amazing mind. He always has an answer to whatever you ask and here you are not ready to give him a chance to share with you the secrets of life which no university teaches to its students. Nobody knows this better than me." Neil considered Ajay to be his professional and personal mentor in life. Jacob went quiet.

Neil's parents had moved to the UK two years ago and now he was all alone in the US. He would spend lots of time with Ajay, sometimes working in the office or at Jacob's house whenever he could find time while Jacob was away at university, especially after the death of Martha. He would always listen very ardently to Ajay's advice.

"You know what, Jacob. Once, your father told me that humans keep stumbling upon the right answers for the wrong questions and the wrong answers for the right questions. I could never understand the meaning of that until today. Now, looking at you, I've just realized that you keep stumbling on the wrong questions and when the right answers are given, you react like you did to your father." Neil's analysis shocked Jacob.

"How can you…." Jacob wanted to protest but Neil raised his hand stopping him midway. He got out of his chair and said to Jacob, "My friend, don't say anything right now, just go home and think it over and try to find out within yourself if you are asking the right questions." To Jacob, at that moment he sounded just like his father.

"But rest assured I'll investigate to see if there really is something bothering your father," Neil said.

Jacob nodded firmly as if to say to Neil, "Please do and I promise that I'll think about what you've said."

Neil was not sure about Jacob's commitment although he had sensed that it was the perfect time for him to try to erase some old beliefs from Jacob's subconscious so that he could be prepared for a new mindset. He had decided to make a serious effort to dismantle the thoughts set in stone in Jacob's mind about the meaning of success in life in order to break the bondage. He knew that this attempt was bound to meet with resistance but a new building required the dismantling of the old which Jacob had constructed in his subconscious over the years.

***

Victor had briefed his FBI contact about the situation with the Waverley Davis network. The FBI had assured Waverley Davis of their full cooperation in unmasking the hackers whilst maintaining complete secrecy. An entire FBI cyber task force was on standby in case of any further attacks. Agent Christopher Ray, a good friend of Victor's, was heading the taskforce.

Meanwhile, at Waverley Davis, new security measures had been introduced to mitigate the cyber threats. The Research and Development departments of all the industrial divisions were asked to sandbox their new programs, even those that were not harmful. But all these measures became absolutely redundant when it was discovered that the malicious code that Victor had trapped and sandboxed earlier was detected on one of the isolated network nodes in the finance division.

"How is this even possible?" Victor had thought when he came to know about it. The FBI was still unaware of this particular attack since it had taken place in an isolated network that was not under cyber surveillance.

"I think we must inform FBI about this latest attack." Farrell was equally puzzled.

"No time, first we'll have to contain it!" Victor shouted. He had seen that the virus had started its work and now outgoing traffic from the affected computer was showing a sudden surge. Victor wanted to configure all the firewalls to block any kind of network traffic from this particular computer. His hands were busy typing the data. Farrell was busy getting login data from the Access Control Server (ACS).

"Victor, it's Neil Anderson who is the user on the computer that's being attacked," Farrell told Victor who was still occupied tightening security and now bore a grim look on his face. He had worked so hard on securing the network against external attacks but now he had discovered that the threat was within Waverley Davis itself. He was enraged.

“We’ve double checked and it’s been confirmed,” Victor was talking on the phone.

“Ajay, I can’t say anything until we’ve concluded our investigations on Neil,” he said.

“Yes sir, I’m well-aware of that and that’s exactly why I’ve decided not to involve the FBI in this matter yet. It’s really hard to believe that he could be responsible for this latest issue but after so many attacks this is the first concrete evidence we have and it must be investigated thoroughly. I’ll prepare a comprehensive report for your review. Thank you, he said putting the phone down. Enough is enough, now they can’t hide from me, he said to himself.

Within the next twenty minutes most of the employees in the finance division, including Neil, had gathered in the conference room. No one knew why they had been asked to this meeting. Neil was asked first to go into an adjacent room. As soon he entered, he felt an unnerving silence. He was shocked to learn that he had been brought there to be polygraphed. What had he done? He asked himself. He was annoyed because everyone knew about his friendship with Jacob and to a great extent with Ajay as well but he was grilled during the polygraph session. He was disgusted by this treatment but released a big sigh of relief as soon as he walked back to the conference room where the others were waiting for their turn, unaware of the proceedings in the other room.

After three hours, Victor and Ajay were looking at the polygraph test with utter disbelief. It showed all the participants had cleared the polygraph and there was no prime suspect in the case so far. Farrell had already watched several days of CCTV footage from Neil's office and had been unable to find anything suspicious.

Ajay picked up the phone and called Neil as soon as Victor had left his office. He wanted to talk to Neil about today's events. He told Neil about the situation in the finance division but chose not to show him the complete picture fearing that Neil would tell Jacob. Actually, he wanted to ask Neil not to tell Jacob anything at all about the attacks or about being polygraphed. Neil was stunned to learn how dangerous the virus on his terminal was. Neil wanted to talk to Ajay as well, to discuss Jacob's issue.

"Ajay, Jacob is concerned about you," Neil said.

"Yes, I know," Ajay said with a touch of cynicism in his voice. "He thinks that he's learnt everything and doesn't need his father to tell him anything." Ajay's reply made Neil think about his own plan to bring about a change to Jacob's way of thinking.

"He's worried about your health, I guess," Neil said.

"I'm perfectly fine, Neil, but I'm the CEO of this firm and there are things which I'm responsible for which include making tough business decisions that no one else can make for me. Not even my son," Ajay said.

"But I don't think there's any harm in sharing a few things with your son. Maybe Jacob could give you few good ideas for future technical products," Neil advised.

"If he'd been so concerned about sharing my burden and been prepared to give me some good technical ideas, he would have joined this firm the day he finished his degree," Ajay said sternly. Neil's advice had offended him a little.

Neil now had another possible reason for Ajay's stress which had been a cause for concern for Jacob over the last few days.

In the entire conversation, Neil had not said a word about Jacob's inability to reconcile with Ajay's wishes or his decision to make his own life instead of joining Waverley Davis but Ajay bringing up these concerns provided Neil with a pretty good idea about the abyss between son and father which was only widening with every passing day. Neil realized that Ajay was pushing Jacob to learn things on a spiritual level which, clearly, Jacob was not yet ready to learn and would need more time to understand.

The same situation applied regarding Ajay's desire for Jacob to join Waverley Davis. He hoped his son would one day become its CEO. In Jacob's mind, rejection of this position was natural. He did not really want the same as his father did for him. He was, after all, more like his mother in that respect than he would ever be like his father.

As his friend, Neil knew just how Jacob's mind was set towards work.

Ajay therefore felt he had failed as a father but could not understand the reasons why.

Jacob, on the other hand, had finished his technical training and had done what his father had asked of him to become a technician in computers.

It seemed that all three felt disappointed on behalf of the others.

Jacob had worked in the Artificial Intelligence Division at Waverley Davis when he was designing an advanced simulation module to manage New York's traffic as part of his final project. This work was a mandatory requirement for the completion of his degree. He had not clearly thought about his future at that time because he was simply focusing on his studies. He had a vision of working at Waverley Davis, starting from the bottom and rising to the top as CTO, the Chief Technology Officer.

On the other hand, Ajay had visualized a different outcome for his son. He saw Jacob as a young CEO sitting in his chair whilst Ajay visited India for longer vacations. Sadly, by continually asking him to join Waverley, Ajay had inadvertently pushed Jacob away. Desperation repels. One of the golden principles of the law of attraction was at work but Ajay had failed to realize it. Neil had seen it and wondered how come Ajay had failed to grasp the obvious.

Now Neil wanted to make Jacob forget worrying about his Dad's health and he had decided how he might make Jacob consider changing his mind about fulfilling at least one of his father's two dreams for him. "Ask and it will be given to you, seek and you shall find, knock and it shall open to you," Neil said suddenly. He had realized that, before changing Jacob's views, preventing Ajay from unwittingly pushing Jacob even further away was a critical imperative. He changed the topic accordingly. "Do you remember teaching me this invaluable lesson?" he asked Ajay who was still trying to understand the sudden change of topic by Neil.

"Do you have something to say?" Ajay asked Neil.

"Ajay, all I want to say is that we can't change a person who is not ready to ask himself if he is ready to be changed. And you've told me a number of times that it's never too late in life to ask this question. Please give

Jacob some time. Let him reach the point where he asks himself this important question," Neil said. Ajay listened to him and was now looking at Neil as if he was meeting him for the first time.

Neil left immediately afterwards. This short interaction between them had triggered memories of Martha in Ajay's mind.

When she was alive, she would find the solutions to his problems with such ease and, on this particular subject, her views would be exactly the same as those that Neil had expressed to him today. He closed his eyes and started to repeatedly play Neil's words in his mind and, within a few minutes, he found a peculiar sort of enlightenment in his consciousness as he began to realize his mistake in this entire affair.

Neil called Jacob as soon as he got to his office and told Jacob that everything was fine as far as the health of his father was concerned and that he must not be worried about his father being displeased with him because of his disappointing behavior. He must accept his father's proposal to join Waverley Davis and become its CEO because this was the reason behind his father's stress. Jacob had not liked what he had heard and rejected Neil's conclusions. Jacob remained convinced it was something else that was responsible for his father's recent stress.

After talking to Jacob, Neil decided to change the perception of Ajay in Jacob's mind as part of his effort to bridge the gap between the two personalities. This was essential if Neil was to succeed in his efforts to rewire Jacob's subconscious and change his belief in life.

***

She was locking the door of her apartment and busy answering her phone

"Yes, I know I'm late but don't worry I'll not miss my mark, I promise," she said putting the door keys in her shoulder bag. She saw a pizza delivery guy knocking on the door two apartments away from her own. As soon as she had passed him and entered the elevator, the pizza delivery guy started to walk towards the door of her apartment, looking cautiously down the corridor. Shifting the empty pizza boxes into his right hand, he reached into his pocket with his left hand. Using a small lock pick kit in no time at all he was inside the girl's apartment which was large and newly decorated. The girl must have had taken it on only recently.

He found what he was looking for in the second room. He pulled a small device out which looked like a small Integrated Circuit (IC). He opened the LAN cabling socket and installed the device there. Then he attached another small device under the top of her computer table. He put it at an angle which concealed it from anyone standing near the table or sitting in the chair. It was a small but powerful listening device. He left the apartment as soon as he had finished his work there. Leaving the building, after getting rid of the pizza boxes in a skip, he activated his mobile which confirmed that both of his devices were active.

Chapter Four

"Reality is a projection of your thoughts Be careful therefore. The things you habitually think about."

Stephen Richards

The mood in the room was very serious.

Ping May was present along with two other people. One was the representative of the Chinese Naval Intelligence Service and the second was the Chinese Political-Bureau's representative, Wu Chin who had met with Ping at another meeting earlier that month.

All three were flicking through different large files in front of them.

"Why haven't we made much progress in the Waverley Davis server matter?" asked Ping May before reminding them that the Party leadership wanted immediate results.

Wu Chin intervened "What's happening at the Central Politburo of the Communist Party? The department wants answers from the Political Bureau and especially from me at the CPC Central Committee."

"I know what the stakes are Wu," he replied.

Wu Chin continued, "As a matter of fact, it was me who devised this plan. Hopefully we can soon finally get some good news about the outcome. It's taking more time than expected and we're having difficulties penetrating the most secure network in the world."

"We're constantly facing stiff resistance from the server we're targeting however the intensity encountered has proved to be somewhat unexpected based on our usual procedures," Ping explained.

"Can you give me anything specific about the progress made so far?" Wu Chin asked again.

"We've already penetrated their perimeter firewalls and gained access to their utility servers, we can't draw any attention to ourselves. The fact that they stay ahead of us is incredible. We remain focused on finding our target, despite the fact that they are constantly changing their internal network configuration and topology," Ping May explained.

"I assume they are fully aware of these attacks?" he asked.

"Yes, they're aware of attacks but they haven't found out our method of collating information yet. Our scanning worm remains hidden in their internal network," Ping replied.

"Well yes, and I suppose that it's only a matter of time until they find that too."

"The FBI's cyber task force has already been involved in this matter." This was Zhang Yong, the naval intelligence person.

"This is a development of real concern," Wu Chin said.

"I had considered this possibility and have prepared a contingency plan for it as well," Ping May said.

"What sort of contingency plan? The FBI will put the entire network under cyber surveillance and they'll be anticipating future attacks," Zhang sounded concerned.

"There are currently ninety three of our cyber task forces under surveillance by the FBI. I'll give each of the ninety-three units heightened activity to distract the FBI. Whilst they are distracted we can sneak into the Waverley Davis military servers but I'm certain things will not come to that." Ping was showing optimism despite the reservations of other two.

"I'm still unable to understand your strategy Ping," Zhang said.

"Isn't that exactly what a secret service is supposed to do Zhang?" asked Ping "I have another asset over there who is assessing the situation with our cyber team and its local contacts. Based on his assessment, I'll make a decision about either escalating or decreasing our efforts."

"The best way to address the FBI problem is to meet our primary objective," Ping continued. "Based on the input of my asset there, we'll have a clearer picture about the odds of success of our current strategy of cyber-attack. If, after assessing the situation, I feel any need to change our line of action, you guys will be informed as well. So far there's nothing new in the strategy."

"Naval intelligence will always be there to assist Ping," Zhang said.

"I have no doubt about that and it's already playing a key role in this plan. We would not have been aware of this American project if it wasn't for our naval intelligence in the first place," Ping praised Zhang's institution. The meeting finished but not before Ping had reassured both Zhang and Wu about the success of the plan.

The Chinese government, however, as a global superpower, was now really concerned about growing international pressure caused by Beijing's claim on the entire South China Sea territory. America was totally opposed to these territory claims. Secretly, the USA armed forces continued to patrol this territory along with its allies in the region. They point blank refused to accept and rejected Chinese claims. Now the US Navy, along with naval ships from other allied nations, regularly showed an armed presence in the area. Using the Freedom of the Navigation charter of the United Nations as cover meant the US could sail these waters legitimately

Diplomatically, this left Beijing in a very vulnerable situation. They were in a very strong position, having rich military resources, but these could not be used. They also knew they had to contain the threat of the US Navy's military project of and its potential impact on the prevailing balance of power in the region. This had created ripples in Beijing. Suddenly, the already troubled waters of the South China Sea had had oil poured upon it.

China had decided to be more active in the secret world of military protocol and they engaged in all forms of espionage and subterfuge.

China had no choice but to initialize a preemptive cyber assault on the USA in an attempt to steal the research concerning the US projects. Furthermore, the Chinese were not members of the United Nations

After the meeting, Ping May thought about the situation for a few minutes and then he asked his assistant to find and contact agent Lee, now active in the USA, as a matter of urgency.

"Report as soon as you get contact," he snapped.

"I've got him on line one now sir," his assistant said, "He's on extension three. Shall I patch him through?"

"Yes, put him on."

"What's your progress, Lee?"

"So far they've had no luck with the primary objective. The main problem is the regular changes in the network security configuration. It seems that they're trying to get back to Fu and his team."

“What’s the risk of that,” Ping asked.

“A plausible scenario and a known risk but no need to be concerned, I’ve planned for that situation,” Lee replied.

“Did the FBI find anything? Ping asked.

“All covers are intact and our network tracing code is still there on the network. It shows that they haven’t found anything,” Lee said.

“Hmm… it looks like they also want to avoid any media exposure of this situation which suits us,” Ping said.

“What are my next orders?” Lee asked.

“Wait for couple of more days. In case of more failures, we’ll move to plan B for which instructions will be passed on to you at the appropriate time. For now, just keep in mind that that is a more kinetic strategy and you’ll have to act fast,” Ping said.

“I think we must continue our current plan a little longer. Any kinetic action will draw unnecessary attention from the US law enforcers and in this particular scenario there is a possibility that the American military will also get involved,” Lee said.

***

Jacob paid a surprise visit to his father’s office two days after he had talked to Neil who had made Jacob realize that he could not avoid his father forever and that eventually he would have to talk to him. The decision to visit was not an easy one for Jacob but, during the last few days, he had realized that he loved his father way more than he disagreed with him.

"I think I crossed my limit and I'm sorry for that Dad," Jacob said to his father. He had to muster a lot of courage to say these words. Jacob had found himself in an unprecedented predicament.

"It's OK, Son. You're entitled to have your own views about life Ajay's reply stunned Jacob. "And you don't have to be sorry, Son." Ajay knew why Jacob was apologizing so he chose not to ask the obvious question.

"I think I've disappointed you more than once in life Dad," Jacob said. This time Ajay realized that Jacob had a lot on his mind and he needed to lessen that burden. Ajay didn't want to punish Jacob any more than his son was already punishing himself.

"First of all, there's no reason for me to consider you to be a disappointment. I have no doubt as to my son's ability to achieve whatever he wants in life. But if you are referring to our disagreement on certain things in life, I think that's natural and if I'm disappointed with anyone, it is with my own self." Ajay had an unfamiliar air of calmness and it was making Jacob nervous.

"Yes. It's true that a couple of dreams I had for you have not been fulfilled but that doesn't mean that it's your fault," Ajay continued. "I taught you to be your own man, to follow your own dreams and then make your own plans to achieve those dreams. Now if your dreams are not reconciled with mine about your future in this company, how can I blame you for that?" Ajay said in the same peculiar calm tone.

When he had arrived at his father's office earlier that day, Jacob had many scenarios in his mind about how this conversation could possibly unfold but what was transpiring at that moment between father and son had not been among those scenarios. He wondered why his father had not realized this obvious fact much sooner instead of continually pushing Jacob to become part of the Waverley Davis management and ultimately it's CEO. "Thank you, Dad, for understanding," Jacob said appreciatively. Finally, he thought, Dad will no longer push me to do that job anymore and I'll be able to concentrate on building my own firm to develop my own secure OS like I've always planned. Little did he know that, at that moment, providence had a whole different future game plan that was about to soon be unveiled?

Ajay observed the change in Jacob's disposition. "Jacob, can I give you a piece of advice for your future endeavors as a business entrepreneur?" Ajay asked.

“Sure Dad. I would love to learn all the secrets of business from the most successful person I know.” Jacob sounded genuinely thrilled.

“Let me share with you one big secret of my life. I was taught to welcome every experience in life, even the disappointments. I acted on these and today look where I am in the global technology market,” Ajay said and Jacob was perplexed.

“Dad how did welcoming disappointments in life lead to your success?” Jacob’s next question surprised Ajay. Something had changed or was changing in Jacob. Unlike earlier, he now wanted to continue this discussion. Ajay was suddenly stunned to see that a change in himself had made such an impact on Jacob as well. On the other hand, Jacob was also pleasantly surprised. So far, nothing that his father had said had made him react the way he would normally would after talking to him on a topic which contained words like “life,” and “experience,” in it.

“What I have learnt in life is that, the way you conduct yourself reveals everything about you.”

Chapter Five

As within,

So without

Diana Cooper

"We must welcome every joy and sorrow as a vital experience in life because we don't know what each experience is going to offer us for the future. Sometimes disappointments trigger a strong urge to bring about a change within ourselves which leads us to recognise our own shortcomings and eventually change our circumstances. I began to embrace my disappointments as lessons instead of shying away from them. Soon enough I was able to fix them myself and address the shortcomings which had brought about those disappointments in my life in the first place. I was able to move forward." Ajay illustrated his life experiences in a very thoughtful way.

This change in Ajay's approach had worked its magic.

"I think I'll be able to make a fresh effort to understand your choices and decisions. And I hope one day I'll discover a far nicer person in my son than I can see in him now," Ajay said with a smile on his face. Jacob was amazed.

"How long does a person keep learning in life?" Jacob asked

"There is no limit, you keep learning all of your life. Lately, I've realized that learning in life never stops. It only comes to an end with our death. However old we are, whatever we go through, it's always possible to be reborn. If each day was a copy of the one before, what a pity! Every breath is a chance to be reborn." Ajay's smile had deepened and Jacob certainly had been given some food for thought. He had never found Ajay's words so full of impact before.

He spent a few more minutes in his father's office then left to meet with Neil before going to a meeting with bank executives to give a presentation about his ideas which would hopefully secure a long term lending agreement with that bank.

"What truly inspires you, Jacob? What's your motivation in life?" Neil asked after Jacob had told him about the earlier discussion with his father. Jacob was puzzled by this unexpected question.

"Innovative ideas, sound strategy and persistent efforts based on that strategy, I guess," Jacob replied looking a little perplexed as he struggled to understand the rationale for this discussion. "Why have you asked that?"

"I want to understand why a person like Ajay Mohan, who you've spent all your life with so far, has failed to become your inspiration in life."

"Look, whatever I am today, it is of his making. He finally accepted that today and now he's fine with me pursuing my own dreams and, you know what, he also gave me some serious food for thought." Jacob's reply put Neil in a feel good mood because he knew for a fact that Ajay would always advise his son in a way that gave give him food for thought. Hopefully, Jacob had the presence of mind to understand that.

Neil smiled because for the first time in his friend's life, he had listened to his father and that meant that something had changed between the two of them. Neil was happy that he was able to break the deadlock and trigger a positive change that was going to bridge the gap between son and father.

"Now it's up to me to not to disappoint him." Jacob sounded determined.

"I suppose your brain is busy planning the best possible strategy to do that already isn't it?" Neil asked.

"You know me too well, old friend," Jacob chuckled. "Yes, that's exactly what's been going on in my head since I left the meeting with Dad earlier," he confessed with a smile.

"Sometimes belief or faith is as important as any business strategy." It was Neil's turn to give his friend some advice. He continued, "Well, at least you're persistent, if nothing else."

"I think persistence is underestimated in one's efforts. I see it as one of the most critical elements for success after that of having a sound strategy," Jacob replied. "You do realize that persistence is just another word for faith, don't you my friend," he said.

At that moment, Neil had a call from his immediate supervisor in the finance department summoning him to an urgent meeting. He hoped Jacob would not leave as he still had something really important to tell him. He was thinking about Clarke, his new girlfriend, and that things had been getting serious between them since they had met for the first time a few weeks ago. Neil was really attracted to her. "Can you give me a few minutes about something personal?" He wanted to tell Jacob about it. Neil knew that his friend would prefer to know first-hand from himself because he knew that if Jacob learnt about Neil's new love match from anyone else, it would literally kill him.

"I can work on this computer here till you come back." Jacob promised not to leave. After almost half an hour after Neil had left for his meeting, there was still no sign of him. Jacob watched the clock tick and stood up, it was getting close to the time for his own meeting with bank executives.

He had no choice. He had to go.

"You know, even Neil has been polygraphed." These were the words he overheard when he passed a group of four finance division employees standing in the corridor gossiping in a small circle.

They continued, "Yes, something really serious is going on and everyone is so hush-hush about it."

"What are all the computer department service engineers doing in the finance department?" they asked. "There are IT guys all over the place."

"Did something bad happen to our computers?" asked another.

That same thought also occurred to Jacob. The group had seen him and dispersed quickly. Everyone was aware of Jacob's friendship with Neil. He continued to walk towards the elevator and soon he emerged from the Waverley Davis finance department enraged and annoyed.

Neil returned to his office from his meeting after around forty-five minutes and gave a big sigh when he saw that Jacob had gone. He wanted to show him Clarke's photo as well as telling Jacob about his feelings for her. "OK. Some other time, my friend," he thought with a smile on his face.

***

In a coffee shop, two girls chatted as they sipped their morning coffee. "How was your meeting?" She continued "I hope no one followed you."

"Don't worry. Everything happened as you said it would, exactly as you said it would, to be precise. He didn't suspect a thing. I was in control."

"Give me the complete details then Natalie. Why did they want to meet me after I'd already finished their job? Why this next meeting now? You know that we never compromise an operation when it's active and the biggest rule is that operatives stay out of the grid, always keep it sterile."

"Well, we have no choice," she replied.

"Tell me why and why compromise this operation as well?" she asked loudly.

"It's about completing another task similar to last task you did," Natalie said. "They want to implant something else in that network and within next four days too," she added.

"How did you respond to that?"

"I played like hard to convince. I told them that it wouldn't be an easy proposition. Operations like these require planning and rehearsal."

"Good. This confirms my suspicions were not misplaced. It's bigger than we first thought. No group can deploy this kind of cyber weapon unless the outcomes are much bigger because now the stakes are so high."

"That explains the compromise and I think it also explains our arrangement," Natalie said.

"Well, Nat, I call it our very important partnership which may one day save our lives as well."

"Oh my God. Is it that serious?"

"Yes, of course." Natalie almost panicked.

"Relax. I'm just saying. It's always safer to have a good friend looking out for you. Isn't it?"

"Yes. You're right, I guess. Please, don't put me in any danger will you," Natalie said.

"It's not you. It's me who's in trouble now with this latest demand of theirs."

"It's just another meeting with some regular guy like you've done hundreds of times before."

"No, this man is different. Sadly, I'll have to do it. I have got emotional feelings for him and even I can't do that."

"Do we have any choice then?" Natalie asked.

"No! I guess we don't .But I'll have to find a way out of this situation."

She stood up from her chair. As she was leaving, she quipped, "Just keep your eyes open. Just in case." Natalie listened to these last words.

Both now standing up, the girls were of the same height with similar relatively thin frames. Their faces were very different though.

"Oh damn," thought Natalie as she walked away from the coffee shop towards her apartment.

***

Jacob reached his office, enraged after learning that he was being kept in the dark about something which had not only stressed his father but had put Neil into some kind of trouble as well.

He was furious at the fact that his best friend had not told him about his polygraph test. More importantly, neither had his father mentioned it.

He was pacing restlessly around his room shaking his head in disbelief. Then, after a few minutes, he started to think about the whole situation. He thought, "You know, even Neil has been polygraphed." He repeated this sentence in his mind again and again. "Even Neil" he thought. Suddenly, he realized, "That means other people have also been polygraphed," he said out loud.

Now he set about analyzing the possible causes for the secretive polygraph. Some financial fraud he thought but then every single scenario he could possibly imagine that entered his head could only to be rejected outright.

He had known Neil since their childhood. Neil was well off and Jacob's Dad absolutely loved him, almost like a son. He would gladly give him whatever he wanted in life. So there is no motive for any crime Jacob thought.

"I ought to ask Neil outright," he thought. Then he remembered earlier in the day, that maybe he had forgotten to mention it. Oh! Then suddenly he remembered their conversation.

He asked me to stay in office after his meeting but I had to leave. This might be the thing he wanted to talk to me about. See, he reasoned, Neil was not guilty of not sharing a secret with him. It was partly my fault and partly his, he mused. Maybe if I telephone Neil on his mobile and ask what the big secret was that he wanted to tell me about earlier, we can discuss this polygraph thingy as well he reasoned.

He waited as the dial tone purred his number. "Hello Neil, it's Jacob, it's me buddy."

"Dude," Neil answered. "You know that I'm really proud of having a buddy like you. Well just listen to this, Jacob, it seems to me that I'm in love with someone," he reported happily.

"Oh, my God that's great, you never mentioned it." Jacob was clearly not ready for this surprise, at least not at a time when he was expecting a very different kind of emotional outburst from him about the near chaos at work.

"I was about to tell you earlier today and that's why I asked you to stay but it got late." Neil was still happy chatting.

Jacob wanted to change the subject by asking, "Why were you polygraphed Neil?" However, he continued to ask about his new girlfriend instead. They spoke at length about his girlfriend, how they had met online and how they had had several great dates.

As he listened, Jacob had to fight very hard to suppress every instinct to ask the question he wanted the answer to.

"Well, has anything else exciting happened with you lately that you want to share with me?" Jacob asked.

"No, buddy. Everything else is just fine."

He put the telephone down and ended the conversation.

After talking to Neil, Jacob once again tried to make sense of his phone call and why Neil had not told Jacob anything about the polygraph tests. He needed to know what the current investigation was about so he was forced to call a few other people at Waverley Davis who he knew from back in his internship days. Somebody should know he thought. Most, it seemed, were operating under strict instructions from higher management not to say anything.

Once again, he walked around his room trying to figure out this riddle.

He began by recalling the first day that he saw his father stressed. That means, he thought, Dad wasn't angry with me or what I had done. The reason must be these polygraphs. All the time his brain was trying to join up the dots.

That's why someone in the corridor mentioned something being wrong with their computers. This level of security, he mused, must be because of Intellectual Property Theft. Maybe it's another scenario, he thought, maybe the leaking of Confidential Financial Data or even military data. Jacob picked up his car keys and left for Waverley Davis. He had decided to ask his father why he had not been told about this situation.

Jacob arrived in Ajay's office.

Ajay was not expecting the visit or the direct question from Jacob. He was surprised by the strong gaze fixed on him as his son waited for an answer that would satisfy him.

"Why did the security team polygraph my best friend then?"

"Who told you? Neil?"

Ajay want to know how much Jacob knew.

"No Dad, he's very loyal to you. He didn't tell me anything," Jacob said. "I came to know about all this by accident." He told his father what he had overheard earlier that day outside Neil's office. "I think you must be well aware of our policy of keeping certain things confidential son so I'm afraid I won't be able to give you an answer to your liking," Ajay said.

"I'm your son, Dad. Neil is my best friend," Jacob protested.

"That's my problem, Son, you're not part of Waverley Davis, are you?" Ajay stated firmly. "You were given a choice to become part of it but you chose not to," he added.

Jacob knew Ajay was right so he could not say anything more. He sat on the chair and remained quiet. He gazed at the floor, thinking and thinking. After a few minutes he stood up and left Ajay's office without saying another word. By the time he reached home, he had made a decision to get to the bottom of this matter which was causing stress to the two most important people in his life.

Unknown to him, the formidable hand of providence had made its move. Jacob's world was about to change forever.

Chapter Six

As above So below

Diana Cooper

Neil and Clarke were meeting once again at their favorite restaurant. Neil had been pleasantly surprised when he had received a call from Clarke earlier that day asking if they could take lunch together. It took Neil only a quick ten minutes to reach the restaurant from his office. He noticed that something had changed about her. Was it her make up? Or the fact that she had a very unusual hair style and her eyes also looked different. For the first time, she was wearing glasses which she had never worn before

These several small changes, although subtle, changed her appearance quite a bit and it was difficult for Neil to recognize her from their previous meetings.

This time, again, she had another hidden agenda.

She had a smile on her face and Neil was smiling too.

She kept thinking she was once again on an assignment. She had been asked to put another virus in the Waverley Davis network using Neil's mobile as a Trojan horse, just like she had accomplished last time.

"Give me your mobile," she suddenly asked Neil. He gave her his mobile wondering what she would do with it. Clarke punched a few keys and raised her left hand up holding the mobile so she could take a selfie.

"That's our first picture together," she commented. Then she took five or six more pictures of them both as she made different poses. Neil smiled as he watched her taking pictures while she struck some really silly poses. She returned his mobile to him and Neil put it back into in his pocket.

"Now do you understand why I dressed like this?" she explained with a peculiar smile on her face.

"Absolutely," Neil laughed.

They had lunch together and chatted about their friendship. Neil left for the office completely unaware that Clarke had put a malicious code on his mobile's chip using his Bluetooth. Neil returned to work.

Clarke called her contact and told him that the mission was accomplished. She had a serious look on her face.

Her eyes scanned the people around her as if anticipating a threat nearby but there was none.

She stood up and headed to the restroom. Entering a cubicle, she locked herself in and looked at her mobile. Her fingers worked really fast on her smart phone. She transferred the same file to an internet cloud via the internet on her Wi-Fi app. She deleted the file as soon as she had completed the transfer. She looked at her watch and let out a big sigh, knowing that she had done her job within the stipulated timeframe.

"It's all there, it's yours to start analyzing," she instructed the other person on the phone.

"Let me know as soon as soon as you come up with a conclusion." She was very strict in her instructions this time.

***

Jacob had been thinking about the possible situation at Waverley Davis and exactly what had happened there. It would have to be bad and had something to do with computers. In addition, it must have involved the finance division and Neil as well. He really had to get to the bottom of this. Where I shall start, he thought to himself, somewhat at a loss as to where to begin.

He realized that not one person inside Waverley Davis would utter a single word so all the facts had been made pretty well secret by now but forgetting about the matter was simply out of the question. He had called a few friends of his father and had tried to make them talk but, as expected, they were simply unaware of anything relevant to his enquiries. By now it was clear to him that he would never get to know what was going on inside Waverley Davis by simply talking to people.

He decided instead to think outside the box.

"I should get into the system in Neil's office to investigate this thing."

However, he realized that would not be possible without hacking into the Waverley Davis network and that was something he would never try. He knew that Victor and all of his team were currently on high alert and would spot him in no time.

"I need to be able to talk to Neil or anyone else who was polygraphed," he thought, "so I need to join the company to find out about Waverley Davis by talking to a few people."

"Yes," he thought, "this is a good idea but how am I going to implement it?"

He also had no idea what he would do if Ajay rejected his application to join the firm now but he would address that problem when he met with his father he told himself.

***

Jenifer was born to a mid-level executive father and a math's teacher mother. She was part of a happy family until her father developed a gambling habit. He started to lose regularly. At first it was easy for him to pay but, over time, he gradually began to incur debts and his actions began to adversely affect his family. Although Jenifer's mother didn't leave her father when she learnt about his debt crisis, she did suffer paralysis brought about by constant mental stress and she eventually lost her job. She had tried to support her husband before she became unable to walk. Jenifer's father then developed serious mental health issues knowing that he could never pay his debts and this led to him eventually committing suicide.

Jenifer was still at school at the time. She was among the brightest students especially in mathematics and computers. She would always draw inspiration from successful people. She loved computers and any kind of communication devices. The computer lab was her favorite place in school. She had developed great acumen very early on by learning many things online. Her biggest dream was to become a successful entrepreneur but her aspirations were shattered by her father's suicide and her mother's paralysis.

Despite all the hurdles, she completed her schooling with distinction and, after gaining a scholarship, she joined a technology college but soon left as she felt there was nothing new for her to learn there. She already knew everything that was being taught and therefore studying there was simply a waste of her time. She looked for a job so that she could support her mother. She started work at a restaurant as a waitress. Her focus in life became limited to taking care of her mother and pure survival. She abandoned her social life but her passion for computers remained the one unchanging constant in her life.

It had been five years since her father committed suicide. Jenifer was still living with her paralyzed mother although now she had found a job as a supervisor in a large hotel.

But now there was a secret side to her life. She had become a professional hacker, developing a reputation within the hackers market. She had not hesitated to put her skills to work in order to earn some extra money by hacking other peoples' accounts. She was connected to different hacker groups through various dark net forums where she had created a digital avatar under a pseudo name. She had not shared any pictures of herself on the internet since she joined the hacker's forum.

Remaining anonymous was the only way to be for hackers and she had easily adapted to it. Due to the nature of her work, she did not trust people readily. Consequently, she didn't have any friends except a girl called Natalie whose original name was Teresa and who belonged to a Mexican family residing in the US. Jenifer had met her in a police lockup when she was arrested for carrying an unauthorized gun. Jenifer was fined by the court but, because of her lack of money, she was sent to prison for four months. Teresa had helped her there, adjusting to life among hardcore women criminals but that was not the biggest attraction to her for Jenifer.

They became good friends only after Jennifer learnt that Teresa was also a computer programmer and had come to the US to seek a better future. Jenifer realized after only a few days that she could trust Teresa and that she was a good computer programmer in low level languages. In her, Jenifer saw a potential partner.

Teresa had been sentenced to thirty months in prison on charges of drug dealing. Jenifer would get out of prison two months before Teresa. She had decided that she would help Teresa disappear so that her former employer would not be able to find her again once she came out of prison. So, when that happened two months later, Jenifer had a new identity for Teresa. Now she was Natalie Jefferson. Jenifer had given her the identity of a missing person who had disappeared a month earlier and who had not yet been found by the police.

Jenifer's circumstances after the death of her father had given her a complex personality. On the surface she was a rude and somewhat mean girl but, deep inside, she was just like her mother; dependable and caring for the people around her. She had taught some hacking skills to Natalie as well, on the condition that she would not contact anyone from her past. Jenifer did not want to stumble upon any surprises if Natalie's former colleagues or employer should come to know who she actually was.

Protecting herself from others had become second nature to Jenifer. She had learnt hand-to-hand self-defense and weapon firing. Over the years, her mother's condition had deteriorated badly and now she needed to be cared for in a physical rehabilitation center for extensive care.

Jenifer was trying to earn some quick money to ensure that she could take good care of her mother. She found this difficult to do on her current income from the hotel with having to pay utility bills and repayment installments for the massive debts her father had incurred. Hacking was the only option but, with the establishment of new cybercrime units in the FBI and police, even that was not an easy task. She had earned some money through writing ransom ware programs but, as the FBI had a special focus on finding cyber ransom seekers, she needed to be careful. When she felt utterly desperate, she would imagine good days ahead, she had told herself not to be a pessimist. But the more she tried the harder it became.

It was during this desperate time that she received a surprise call from an unknown person promising a large amount of money for a relatively small task. She was tasked to implant a malicious code into the mobile of someone called Neil who was an employee at the headquarters of a multi-billion dollar technology firm. She adopted a different name for the task and met with Neil as Clarke. She pretended to be his friend and dated him several times to gain his trust but it was still a risky proposition and she could be caught in the act. She had later come up with a different plan and was able to give Neil an infected phone.

Life had never the same for her after that day.

She had not been told about the exact purpose of that malicious code yet she became intrigued to see what it was capable of and why an anonymous person had wanted it implanted inside the computer terminal of one of Waverley Davis' employees was anybody's guess.

She had received the money for services rendered very quickly via a subterfuge as was often the case in such matters. She made a few more discreet enquiries about the purpose of the Malware but, despite asking several times, she was always promised an answer later. As she was mistrustful by nature and for her own piece of mind, she made a copy of the code and put it in her personal diary. She would ask Natalie, she said to herself, she would probably know.

Initially, she had sought assistance from other friends but, with Natalie's help, discovered that the Malware code was no virus at all but an intelligent code capable of fooling internet security mechanisms and scanning the network on both sides of any secure firewall protection. Neither had ever seen a code like this before but both knew that the sponsors had put a lot of effort and resources into its creation.

In short, it was a perfect cyber weapon which, when active, could help any proficient hacker team with a mind to, to control its target network.

She had become even more intrigued after learning the functionality of the malicious code. Taking control was the obvious answer but she wanted to be clear about the end game. Her natural hacking instinct forced her to investigate further into this matter.

By accident, she had become part of the cyber war between her unknown benefactor and the Waverley Davis Security Division. Soon she discovered that whoever had given her that code did not want to take control of the Waverley Davis Security Division's network but was looking for some specific node on that network. This whole situation was becoming more enthralling to her with every passing day but she still did not know the hacker's end game.

What she witnessed in the coming days was something unprecedented to her. It was an intense cyber war between very capable hackers and equally capable defenders. Soon she learnt that the Waverley Davis Security Division network was a cyber-fortress. Not an easy target by any means. She monitored the methods adopted by the hackers for a few days and then she realized that the Waverley Davis Security Division cyber-fortress was not impregnable after all. She saw their firewalls being breached by hackers. Had she not intervened, they would have penetrated into the utility network of the Waverley Davis Security Division. She had acted because she had still not found the answers to any her of her questions about what the hackers actually wanted from the Waverley Davis Security Division. For her, the only way to stay relevant in this war was to maintain the status quo and not let anybody win decisively and this is exactly what she did in the days to come.

Natalie had also become involved in the tussle when Jenifer was asked to meet Fu Wang to be assigned another task for which payment would be greater than had been received for the previous job. Jenifer had seen enough evidence to realize that someone wanted her to be a pawn in their game. Her survival instinct forewarned her about the approaching storm. She devised a strategy for survival by asking Natalie to impersonate her and meet with Fu Wang. Natalie was reluctant at first but agreed to the meeting as she knew that her own survival was dependent on Jenifer's.

After meeting with Fu Wang, Natalie told Jenifer about the latest demand of her mysterious benefactor. She was being asked to implant another malicious code on Neil's mobile using his Bluetooth. Instructions were specific this time. She was given a very short time in which to complete the task. The intrigue and urge to know the unknown had drawn her into a dangerous web. She made a copy of this code too, again in her diary. She needed to analyze it and get onto the Waverley Davis network to maintain the balance in this war so that she can stay relevant and learn more.

***

Jacob was once again in Ajay's office with a proposal that was not easy for Ajay to accept but for him to reject it was also not an option.

Although Ajay had an idea why Jacob had come up with something like this, he had not a clue what to do. Jacob had asked his father to make him a part of Waverley Davis as he had always wished. Ajay knew that Jacob's request was motivated by his desire to find out the reasons for those polygraph tests.

Should he welcome Jacob and let him help or not? His decision would give Jacob's life a final and irreversible turn and making a decision knowing this made it a difficult task. Ajay had always visualized Jacob sitting in his chair and now, when Jacob was finally ready to fulfill his father's dream, Ajay was not sure if Jacob's commitment was for the long term or whether he was being driven by a fleeting rush of emotions. Finding the answer to this question was vitally imperative before Ajay made any decision.

"I want to know if he's in for real, for the long-term. What do you say about his sudden change of heart?" Ajay asked Neil who was in his office at Ajay's request. Ajay had sent Jacob back home after listening to his proposal.

"Ajay, as far as I can recall, I don't remember Jacob ever making any commitment without giving it serious thought. If he's willing to join Waverley Davis, this is a welcome development I guess and you must welcome him." Neil was surprised as well but was also happy for Jacob and pleased that now they would become coworkers as well.

"I know but what's the guarantee that he will not leave the company as soon as this crisis is over?" Ajay asked.

"Ajay, you've taught me and others here that every second in our life is a chance to change ourselves and rediscover our destiny. As an old friend of Jacob's, I'm positive that he's found that second of change in his life. Or in Martin Luther King Junior's dictum, we are not able to see the whole staircase right now but we must take the first step with faith and so we must help Jacob to do the same." Neil's contribution caused Ajay to pause in deep thought.

"OK," Ajay finally broke the silence, "I'll accept his request, Neil. I'm ready to take the first step. Not because I have found the answer to my question but because of the fact that the other option is to just lose him forever."

"Ajay, you've made this possible through your own subconscious. Your attraction for Jacob was more powerful than his vision to be a successful entrepreneur," Neil said.

"If that's so, it's not given me the kind of happiness and fulfillment that I was hoping for." Ajay said. "More than anything, I wanted him to succeed in life. I didn't demand my victory at the cost of his defeat he added.

"But wouldn't you like to be happy and proud at the same time?" Neil asked. "Now you've made your mind up to accept his request, I'd suggest that you use your powerful imagination to visualize his success here," Neil said with a smile on his face.

At that moment, Ajay once again thought about how invaluable a friend Neil was to Jacob. Always there for him. As a matter of fact, he had spent more time with his son than he himself was able to spend.

Jacob and his father had further discussions around the dinner table that night.

"What did you decide, Dad?" Jacob asked, feeling goosebumps all over.

"Well, before answering that question I'd like to ask you something first and I'd like to have an honest reply." Ajay's remarks unsettled Jacob even further. "What really made you change your mind overnight? Is it me not telling you about the polygraph tests or the other things going on at Waverley Davis or do you really want to be part of my team?" Ajay asked, keeping his tone sober.

"Dad, it's my belief that nothing in this universe moves without some kind of motivation. Both science and logic agree on that. Yes, it's true that your stress, the polygraph incident and Neil's advice have been those motivational forces. But Dad, for the last few days I've felt a strong urge within to be with you," Jacob said. "Dad! I want to know you better. I've seen Neil and I'm amazed how much he's changed since he joined Waverley Davis."

Ajay was overwhelmed by Jacob's unexpected reply. He had thought of dozens of possible answers that Jacob might give but this one was not among them. Ajay tried to remember how much time he had spent with his son and felt a sense of disappointment as his conscience told him that, however long it was, it had not been enough. He began to recall all those events in Jacob's life when Ajay had not been there with him. Jacob was close to his mother but he had always idealized his father as a model of success. Martha had always told Ajay of a simplistic formula for success. Jacob had converted that simplistic formula into his own template for success.

"Jacob," Ajay said earnestly and embraced his son. Both hugged each other as if they had been living in two different worlds and were meeting after a long time apart.

"Welcome to Waverley Davis, Son," Ajay said with tears in his eyes.

"Thank you Dad," and Jacob's demeanor was no different to his father's.

Chapter Seven

"Manifesting is a lot like making a cake. The things needed are supplied by you, the mixing is done by your mind and the baking is done in the oven of the universe."

Stephen Richards

It had now been more than three weeks since the last penetration into the Waverley Davis Security network. Jenifer's intervention had ensured that the network had remained safe. Perimeter defense breaches were not a matter of concern as far as her efforts to maintain a status quo in this cyber war was concerned. On the other hand, the Chinese were really surprised how none of their attacks had been completely successful despite the fact that they had a clear picture about the internal network topology of the Waverley Davis Security internet architecture. After repeated failures in their attempts they had decided to test a new cyber weapon but still no attack had been successful because of Jenifer's intervention. This had caused palpable panic among the Chinese intelligence, navy and political leadership.

"Have you considered the diplomatic cost of this plan Ping?" Li Jingling, a senior Pollitt-Bureau leader, asked.

Ping May was there to present an alternative line of action to the top Chinese leadership by which to extract or destroy the secret US weapon. There were around twenty people in the hall sitting around both sides of a long table. His plan involved obtaining by any means, including violence and kidnapping, the data required.

"A kidnapping of this scale would not go unnoticed. All the USA law enforcers would be looking for a victim like that," another voice was heard raising objections to Ping May's plan.

"Indeed. Every aspect and possible outcome has been carefully analyzed by myself and my team. First of all, let me make it clear that not taking any action is not an option at all. We've tried and tested multiple cyber-weapons. The suggestion of using kinetic force is the option of last resort and I don't think there is anyone here who will disagree with that," Ping May said firmly.

"Just how have you calculated the odds of success of this Plan-B of yours?"

"What makes you so sure that it will deliver?" yet another question was thrown in.

"The idea is to firstly kidnap Victor's family and then force him to deliver to us the information we require under duress," Ping May explained. Many whispers whisked around the hall.

"But how does it address the problem of the US law enforcers, Ping?" someone else asked.

"The operation will be carried out by three teams each hitting their mark in a synchronized plan," Ping explained. "Our resources are already there on the ground preparing for the operation as we speak and awaiting instructions to hit their marks. Jinn Wu from the Chinese embassy will be supervising the operation from there," he added. There was silence in the room.

"No one here has any doubt about your or your men's preparation for this operation but I think we must debate the ways we can avoid any serious diplomatic fallout from such an undertaking," The most senior member reiterated the concerns of Li Jingling. "What you said earlier in this regard presents no solution to this question and you know the stakes here. Without finding a satisfactory answer to this question, we can't approve your plan," he added. All eyes were on Ping May who showed no signs of worry.

"Diplomatic concerns are always amongst the top considerations in the planning of such operations. And this particular operation is no exception to the rule. Officially, our target will be kidnapped and killed by a North Korean agent who, if required, will also confess to his crimes." Ping May's plan once again brought deadly silence into the hall.

"What if the North Koreans reject him as being one of their agents?" Li Jingling asked.

"They will try but will not do anything about it because, as you can see in the files you have been given, the agent deployed on this mission was actually born in North Korea and remained there until very recently." Ping May unveiled his secret weapon in the USA. Lee's details were indeed there in the files stating he was a North Korean citizen. This fact was partially true. Lee had been born in North Korea but, at the age of fifteen he had come to China. Ping May had been a mid-level ranking officer in the People's Liberation Army in China at that the time. He had seen the potential in Lee and had trained him in all the skills he now possessed.

"This will make it impossible for the USA to recognize him even if they tried," Ping May added.

"And what would our strategy be if Washington chose to retaliate?" Li Jingling asked

"Where would they retaliate, North Korea or China? And what kind of retaliation?" Ping May countered.

"The USA are over nineteen trillion dollars in debt. They can't even afford to send troops to the conflict zones that their interventions have created in the Middle East. Thinking about a possible full-fledged retaliation over a kidnapping or murder is just too farfetched.

The Chinese are already superior in information technology. The Americans, however, do have the edge in military matters but if we achieve our target through this plan, China would put that technological superiority to an end, at least in naval power projection capabilities. This mission is important not only for our national defense but also for regional stability." He analyzed the USA's vulnerability which was clearly advantageous to his plan and also explained the plan's rationale.

"I think Ping May has made everything pretty clear to all of us. We must accept his plan as there's no real alternative," the senior member announced and everyone nodded their heads in approval. The mission was to go ahead. Ping May was happy that a big hurdle had been removed and that he could contact Lee and Jinn Wu as quickly as possible to finalize the last remaining tactical details and put the mission in motion.

***

The two blonde haired girls sat opposite each other at the back of a small coffee outlet at Grand Central Railway station next to the world famous oyster bar.

"I never thought that I'd be facing a situation like this." Jenifer was clearly panicking.

"Well, this is not just a situation; it is an outright existential crisis for us" Natalie seemed more fretful than assured.

Jenifer continued, "I gave them your picture as part of the agreement to conceal my true identity." She had exchanged the picture previously not realising that she would meet Neil again." This meant that they would have to swop places again. Next time, she would have to meet Neil.

The Chinese contingent had Natalie's picture believing it to be Jenifer, Fu Wang's local contact who was working on Neil. Lee had also bugged Natalie's apartment while Jenifer's place was still secure. The problem with this deception was that it was impossible to know how long it would last. Jenifer had devised the plan to use someone else to impersonate her after she had been asked by her unknown benefactor to work with Fu Wang's group. She had heard many horror stories which often ended badly.

Jenifer needed to get to relative safety from impending threats from at least a safe distance.

"I think this is the time for us to disappear," she said. "Soon, if this goes pear-shaped…."

"All hell will break loose," Natalie suggested. "We'll create our own exit plan." They had got to get out of this operation.

Jenifer rejected her suggestion instantly.

"I think if we're to survive this situation, then we need to play each scenario carefully from here on in. Besides there's zero possibility that I'll have to meet Neil and Fu Wang both at the same time so that's something I intend to use to my advantage."

"True, but you're a very close friend of Neil's. How can you avoid seeing him and if the Chinese are monitoring him, there's always a possibility of you being spotted."

Natalie warned Jenifer about a clear and present danger which unnerved Jenifer. She was not thinking with her eyes open.

“I think it’s time to end my affair with Neil,” she said.

“He’ll be heartbroken,” she thought. Well, that’s a small price to pay for something that will considerably improve the odds of our survival. “You can keep meeting with Fu or anyone else and maintain your cover,” she told Natalie

“That’s the trouble, my friend. That’s not your choice. It was part of your task to pretend to be his girlfriend and I’m not certain that task is over yet. You’ve already met with him twice regardless of whether you wanted to meet him or not. How then do we know that there will be not a third time?” Natalie said. Jenifer wore a sign of frustration on her face.

“You can avoid that third meeting but you’ll have to act on my plan,” Natalie said.

Meanwhile, Jenifer was still lost in her own thoughts.

“No Nat! We’ll stay here and face whatever is about to unfold,” Jenifer said. “Running is not an option for hackers because a hacker is always online, always present. We’re always easy to find if someone looks closely enough. Besides that, if we run we’ll draw unnecessary suspicion from everyone involved.”

The status quo that is being maintained by me in this war will not be lost either she thought secretly.

“There’s no end in sight and time is a luxury we don’t have. We don’t even know what their target is in Waverley Davis,” Natalie said.

Jenifer thought then commented, “Time is not a critical variable here; it’s maintaining the plausibility of our identities which is critical right now. We’ll have to maintain our respective covers at all costs. Once we get to the bottom of this cyber war we’ll be able to make more realistic decisions about our future course of action.”

“Well then to achieve that, we’ll have to examine this second malicious code our Chinese friends have planted on poor Neil’s mobile,” Natalie said.

“Poor Neil?” they both chuckled and Natalie punched Jenifer in the arm with a smile on her face.

“That’s a brilliant, even an excellent idea,” Jenifer said and grabbed the keyboard. Her fingers ran really fast with her eyes fixed on at the screen.

“Have you got the diary with you?” knowing the code was in Jenifer’s diary. “Yes, right here,” she replied. They both got busy typing, pointing, gesturing looking at the screen. They spent the next five hours trying to understand the true nature of that code and what they found left them with even more questions.

“Many years ago, I came across news stories highlighting Chinese attempts to develop something like this,” Natalie said. “I never imagined that one day I’d see this thing developed and in full operation,” she added.

“What in the files at Waverley Davis is making these Chinese so determined and behaving crazy like this?” Wish I could get to the bottom of this mystery, she contemplated.

“Well, it’s no real big surprise for us is it? We both well know about the portfolios of Waverley Davis. They specialize in military firmware. Now it’s evident that whatever the Chinese are after, it has great strategic value for them which means it has great strategic value for us also, when I say us, I mean this country, the USA.” Natalie had chanced upon something unknowingly.

“It means sooner or later the FBI and CIA will also be part of this thing,” Jenifer said.

“This will also be monitored by various cyber commands of the US military,” Natalie added to Jenifer’s observation.

“A storm is brewing,” Jenifer muttered.

“This program works on the premise that involves some dangerous interrupts being called to affect the functionality of certain functions of CPUs and random memories,” Natalie said pointing at the monitor screen.

"How badly this will affect them is not clear from here but for sure it is just too sophisticated. We'll need more time to fully understand this cyber internet type weapon."

Jenifer then remembered, "The Iranian nuclear program was allegedly sabotaged by a worm virus a few decades ago during the Bush Administration. They used a worm very similar with the help of Stunt virus. The virus is Stuxnet version 2.0."

"What in heaven's name was that?" asked Natalie

"Stuxnet is a malicious computer worm believed to be a jointly-built American-Israeli cyber weapon program, although neither state has confirmed this openly. However, there were US officials who claimed that this worm was developed during the Bush administration to sabotage Iran's nuclear program with what would appear to be a long series of unfortunate accidents.

The Stuxnet virus specifically targets programmable logic controllers (PLCs) which allow the automation of electromechanical processes such as those used to control machinery on factory assembly lines and amusement rides or centrifuges like those used for separating nuclear material. It works by targeting their operating systems and networks and then the virus seeks out moving, spinning mechanical parts. It can then cause motor or server destruction on industrial systems by causing the fast-spinning centrifuges to tear themselves apart.

Back in the 1970s, Stuxnet, or at least it was rumored, reportedly ruined almost one-fifth of Iran's nuclear centrifuges. The consequences set their nuclear capability back for nearly twenty years by ensuring that the hardware control mechanism of their centrifuge machines was compromised," explained Jenifer, "and in my opinion this one looks almost identical to Stuxnet 2.0."

"Really?" Natalie was curious.

"I don't think I'd be able to help them anyway," she reasoned, "because it would take me days to understand this virus worm let alone build a response and by then this damn code would already be there in their network, I guess." Now Jenifer was reconsidering Natalie's plan to get off the radar for a while.

***

FBI's Christopher Ray gave his latest findings to Waverley Davis. He was speaking to Victor and Jacob and he held a large sheet of graph paper in his right hand. He spoke, "Even his polygraph report is clean." He was still in state of shock but he was referring to Neil.

"It surprised us both," Victor said, meaning himself and Jacob.

"Remember that many expert criminals have fooled the polygraph tests before," Christopher said.

"Wait, are you suggesting Neil is some kind of criminal?" Jacob protested.

"It's not me. You've seen the forensic report presented by Victor," Christopher replied.

"Believe me, it's as difficult for me to fathom Neil's choices as he is also my best friend."

"What if someone else has tried to frame him? Someone might have," Jacob said thinking about another possibility.

"That might be the case but we'll have to act according to the law here Jacob," Christopher said. "Only further investigations will unmask the truth but, unfortunately, this has to be the starting point," he added.

Jacob had started to work at Waverley Davis but not in his father's office. He had joined as cyber architect and was working in close quarters with Victor and Farrell. He was amazed by the scale and sophistication of the attacks which were being mounted on the Waverley Davis network. He was also impressed by the work done by Victor and his team. Jacob had seen the obvious fact that lately the attacks were being externally mounted but there was certainly also suspicious activity going on by someone from within the network.

The access logs were thoroughly examined and it was discovered that in every attack the timings of both the internal and external activities were always identical. However, after further investigation, Jacob was also able to conclude that there was no link between these peculiar activities. This was a paradox.

The internal activity was actually responsible for the continuation of these attacks despite the many changes done by Victor in network topology and internal IP address schemes. So, it was obvious that in order to prevent the external network attacks, internal malicious activity had to be stopped. Jacob asked Victor to start investigating everyone passively with the help of their own cyber investigation software toolkit.

He, Victor, did not want to want to give away any sign of this secret investigation and by doing so alert the enemy insider. To that end all mobile phones, tablets, Wi-Fi pods and other handheld devices were the particular focus of this investigation. Victor realized that he had missed a big opportunity here, to strengthen the internal security.

After further investigations, Victor's security team had reached a conclusion and they reported back to Ajay that they knew who was involved in these attacks and that the final suspect involved in these hacking attacks was unfortunately Jacob's best friend Neil. This devastated Jacob and, to an extent, his father as well. Neil's involvement was first reported to Ajay by Victor. He had not wanted to tell Jacob considering his close friendship with Neil.

It was not an easy proposition for Ajay to comprehend this newly learnt fact. He was in a state of complete disbelief and was worried about how Jacob would react after learning this news.

Victor demonstrated that they had found something on Neil's mobile which contained a hitherto unknown malicious code. Victor also revealed that the code had more than one function. Its primary function was to scan the network and send information in encrypted format to a predestined IP address while its secondary function was to launch an attack after creating various copies on the network node. He was able to decipher this by analyzing the code and the results of the last attack initiated by this code from one of the finance division's servers. Ajay informed the FBI agent as soon as it was confirmed by Victor that Neil was indeed the perpetrator. Earlier, Ajay had succeeded in keeping the FBI at bay but two days ago he was asked by the office of the Secretary of Defense to fully involve the FBI in this matter. Naval Cyber Command had detected an unusual surge in network activity on the Waverley Davis network and had found out about these attacks some time ago.

Ajay was informed that the decision to involve the FBI was made on principle by all the stakeholders involved, including leading military in the Pentagon and the White House. The FBI had launched its own investigations as well. All the findings of Victor and his team were shared with them and they conducted interviews with some people, including Victor and Farrell, as part of their preliminary investigations.

Jacob was last to know about this development because he was reacting just as Ajay had expected him to react.

"Jacob, I'm sorry but Christopher is going to take Neil in for further investigation. He's our main suspect and as such is under federal arrest. The FBI wanted to know more information, hence the investigation into Neil."

"No charges will be sanctioned against him unless we establish his direct link with the hackers. And right now, we just want to find out if he had any active role in these attacks." Christopher explained his plan. "But we must be absolutely clear that this is a matter of national security."

"OK. But can I talk to him for a minute before you take him?" Jacob asked Christopher

"Yes, of course," he replied.

Although Jacob had been allowed to talk to him before his arrest, he wasn't sure what he should ask Neil.

"Neil, what does Waverley Davis mean to you?

"It means everything to me, my life, and my future," Neil said with a look of sincerity, "Why?"

"Why what?" Neil asked still struggling to find any sense in Jacob's question.

"Why have you become complicit in a plan to destroy the organization and the family which gave you everything you have today?" By now, Jacob was losing control of his emotions.

"Please Jacob. Stop this game of riddles. This is just conjecture so far, what has happened." For the first time, Neil's voice was louder than Jacob's.

"Come with me." Jacob decided to show Neil what Victor had discovered. Neil followed him to Ajay's office where he was about to be met with the biggest shock of his life.

***

"It means that this girl is responsible for our failure so far," Ping May said on his mobile talking about the update report from Lee.

"I think she has to be extinguished. She must go, the sooner the better. She can create serious trouble for us." Lee advised Ping May to eliminate Jenifer after hearing her recent discussion with Natalie via his listening device planted under the top of Natalie's computer table.

"What do we know about her and her agent partner and who is more dangerous for us?" Ping May countered.

"In fact," he said, "they are both bad news for us. They're loan agents and working as a team." Lee was excited but also very cautious as to why Ping had not so far given him the go ahead for the assassination of both girls.

"You've told me that neither of them have any way to help Waverley Davis against our new weapon, right?" Ping asked Lee to reconfirm the fact he had told him earlier in his report.

"Yes sir. That's what they've said," Lee confirmed.

"We need to be sure about this and if it is the case, then we can deal with them afterwards. For now, we need to focus on our real target. That's the person who manages their network security. Killing two girls in New York will create suspicion which we must avoid for now," Ping said.

"Later on, I'm thinking about owning and running them both, they've great potential as cyber troopers. It's time to make the ancient philosopher Sun Tzu proud," he added with a slight hint of cynicism in his voice.

"Never mind Sun Tzu," he said, "this will be recognized at presidential level. This will be recognition from Xi Jinping himself."

"Goodness, really?"

"Yes, really," he said.

Lee got the thread of what Ping was implying and now had a smile on his face as well. He looked at his laptop where the digital version of a report file was showing a picture of a family of three. A father, mother and their son at the school the child went to. Lee had been tailing his target since he had got the final signal from Ping.

"Indeed politics has no heart beating in its chest," he muttered whilst looking at the next slide on his computer where a close-up picture of an eight year old boy appeared. "Nothing personal young man, just another assignment," he whispered to himself.

On the screen, a third slide was displayed featuring a photo of Victor.

***

"What is this?" he asked. "Some kind of joke?"

This was Neil's reaction after hearing the detailed charge sheet against him which included details of his alleged role in multiple cyber-attacks on his employer from the FBI agent. The FBI had put together a large dossier on Neil. "I think you know the answer to that question very well Neil, we take our job very seriously." Christopher's reply was firm and cold.

Although Neil was confident and felt fairly calm because he had done nothing wrong, at least not knowingly, he clearly felt uncomfortable thinking about the possible outcome of this case. Moreover he imagined his parents learning of that news.

"I think I should be given a chance to explain my end of story as well," Neil said protesting against his arrest.

"Neil! That will only be possible if you cooperate with us. Right now everything is pointing at you being complicit in this entire episode," Christopher said. Shaking his head, Neil looked at Ajay and Jacob.

He was asked to hand over his mobile and his company tablet to the FBI. Everyone in his department saw him in handcuffs with his head down being escorted by two New York police officers.

Christopher registered his arrest and the allegations made against him in an FBI memo.

For Jacob, it was not a comfortable scene and his thoughts were clearly divided. He was enraged by the fact that a person he had known for so long had betrayed his and his father's trust but at the same time he was consciously trying to remember all of his interactions with Neil over the last year when he might have shown any sign of dissatisfaction towards Waverley Davis. He could find no motive for Neil's crime.

Ajay was even more perplexed by Neil's arrest. The moment Neil had walked into his office along with Jacob before his detention. Ajay's sixth sense had told him that Neil was innocent. Ajay knew that he had been used by someone but he was furious at the fact that Neil had somehow allowed somebody to do that to him. He had been trained to avoid seduction and temptations but Ajay had no reason to believe that was a possibility because he knew Neil was not involved in an affair. At least, that is what he had believed. Neil had not told Ajay about Clarke. He had hesitated to do so because he wanted to tell Jacob first.

That decision had cost him dearly.

Christopher was standing next to a big wall mounted LED TV where pictures of various Waverley Davis employees were being displayed. He was giving briefings about these employees to the FBI team. He explained to them why the protection of each one of these people was necessary. He had been tasked to solve the Waverley case as a high priority. Military authorities in the US wanted to see this case resolved ASAP.

Diplomatic channels were also being activated but to make those efforts effective, the US government needed a smoking gun pointing towards the Chinese and it was the FBI's task to provide the diplomats with that weapon. So far, the FBI had just apprehended an American national who, despite being cooperative, had not been able to provide any kind of lead. Everyone in his contact page on Facebook and phone book had already being put under watch.

In order to avoid unnecessary panic, these people were not told about the monitoring exercise. Christopher was hoping Neil's co-conspirator would be drawn out into the open through one of these people and there was also a possibility that one of these contacts was behind the attacks. He needed to protect them but also investigate them at the same time. In the first phase he had decided to interview all those who had contacted or were contacted by Neil.

"We won't know if the person we are protecting is a potential victim or a possible perpetrator so we'll have to maintain as much secrecy as possible," Christopher told his squad. "Keep your eyes open but do not preempt any situation unless you feel that the threat is eminent. Right, are there any questions?" he asked.

With that, he concluded his presentation and the FBI Squad was dismissed while he kept staring at all those faces in the photo collage looking out from the giant LED screen.

Victor's face was also there among those faces. He was completely unaware of the threats he was about to face in the coming days.

Chapter Eight

For verily I say unto you, that whosoever shall say unto this mountain, be thou removed, and be thou cast into the sea; and shall not doubt in his heart, but shall believe that those things which he say shall come to pass; he shall have whatsoever he sayeth.

Mark 11:23

Jennifer spoke after examining the print-out in front of her for a short while.

“They’re not trying to steal it. They’re looking to cripple the entire cyber infrastructure of Waverley Davis but why, because this graph of figures just doesn’t make any sense.” Jenifer was shocked and mystified by the true nature of the code.

“This Waverley Davis thing is getting messier with every passing minute,” Natalie remarked.

Jenifer nodded her head, agreeing with Natalie.

“There must be a reason. Something must have changed,” Jenifer said, after thinking for a while.

“I think by now the Chinese must have realized that they can’t penetrate into the Waverley Davis network so they must have adopted the second best option,” Natalie guessed. Natalie was right in her guess.

The actual Chinese plan was to cripple the entire node points in the Waverley Davis network with the help of this new worm so that barriers could be removed and the complete network detail could be gathered. So far, both the Chinese and Jenifer were only able to see the part of the network that lay between the internal interface of the perimeter firewall and the external interfaces of each internal firewall which were installed to protect each division’s network independently.

This meant that each division had a second tier defensive mechanism so this prevented this type of worm intrusion. Thankfully, as yet, they had not found a way through these internal firewalls. It was impossible to hack from outside the network. Now it seemed the only way to gain access to any particular department was through its respective employee's computer terminal. This method was exactly what they had used to copy the information on Neil's mobile including the Malware. This enabled the Chinese to scan the complete network of the finance division. The second worm was made to address this problem. It was designed to do a lot more than just by-pass the perimeter firewalls. Exactly how still remained a mystery to them. So far, Jenifer and Natalie were unable to understand this part of its operation.

Big multinational companies like Waverley Davis adopt secure server space for secure backup location on and off internet storage for storing strategically important data. By having a secure complete reserve system backup then Waverley Davis would be back operational in a few hours so it made no sense for the Chinese to destroy their local back up. They would need to completely destroy both the internet storage and the local server. Both girls mused that they therefore needed to know exactly what the Chinese were after.

"Maybe they are trying to slow down the Waverley Davis research," Natalie said.

"Well, that's plausible," Jenifer replied.

"Jenifer has finally agreed with me on something," thought Natalie.

Jenifer at the time was thinking of different ways to come up with some method of her own to stop this new code from working. This was not impossible especially with Natalie on her team. Perhaps she could program a low level language to work using computer dialogue. To successfully do this, she needed more time and she was not sure how much of it she had. Unknown to her, this had already been taken care of by FBI.

For now, all she could do was to stay inside the Waverley Davis network and continue her earlier work there.

***

Jacob sat at the dining table at home chatting to Ajay.

"This doesn't make any sense, Dad. I can't understand why Neil would do something like this."

It had been three days since Neil's arrest and Jacob was still unable to find any possible motive which could have made Neil complicit in such a high profile cyber-attack. "I don't think he did that, well at least not with his consent." Nothing Neil did had made sense since that since that fateful day. Maybe, it was because Neil had a firm understanding and belief on all things related to the Law of Attraction and other universal laws.

Ajay had refused to accept the charges against Neil. However, he could not intervene as the FBI was involved.

“I promise I’ll get to the bottom of it. Clearly he’s been framed by someone,” Jacob said.

“Do you think someone inside Waverley Davis is involved?” Ajay asked.

“I don’t know Dad but let’s see what the FBI comes up with.” Jacob was desperate to know the truth but actually had no workable plan to find it on his own. They had no other option but to rely on the help of the FBI.

Straight after dinner, Jacob got an urgent call on his mobile and immediately a worried look appeared on his face. “OK. I’m on my way,” Jacob said.

“Is it anything serious?” Ajay asked.

“Yes,” he said, “it’s Victor. It seems the hackers are active again.”

Jacob reached Waverley Davis as quickly as he could.

Having told Jacob about the activity on their network by hackers, now both Victor and Jacob were in the control room where Farrell and other members of Victor’s team were busy trying to prevent any cyber access. Although the intensity of the attack was a lot lower this time, the hackers were persistent.

This seemed unusual to both Jacob and Victor. Jacob had studied the attack pattern of the previous violations. This attack was similar but not identical to the other attacks. Suddenly, there was a surge in the hackers' activities. Minutes later some of the hackers had managed to bypass the perimeter firewall and were now trying to compromise the email server of the Waverley Davis mainframe server. This attack however was almost identical to one which they had mounted on their access control server a few weeks ago.

"What are they trying to do?" Jacob asked.

"Farrell!" Victor shouted, to gain his attention.

"This attack has two different sources. I think they've upped the mode of attack and want to test our network again."

"Are you certain about the two different sources?" Jacob enquired

"I'm positive," Farrell replied whilst his hands remained busy on the keyboard.

"They want to compromise the email server in the hope of finding some clues. Surely, these fools must know that this isn't the primary email server and can be taken offline at any minute without disturbing the users," Victor said after seeing the concerned look on Jacob's face.

"I think there's someone else in the network as well as these other hackers and it looks like it's another unidentified hacker," Farrell said suddenly.

"Are you sure?" Jacob asked.

"I think so. This is definitely our mystery first hacker I told you about," Victor said. He was in fact as intrigued by this unknown second hacker as he was exasperated by those other hackers.

"Wow! They're at work again," Farrell said.

"What do you mean?" Victor asked.

"Some of the access control rules have been added to the email server just to make it more difficult," Farrell replied.

"That means whoever this hacker is, they're able to penetrate our servers at will," Jacob said, distress raising his voice.

"Don't worry, Jacob. Farrell is working on tracking them and we'll soon have them unmasked."

Once again, Waverley Davis' vital server was saved by this unknown hacker. Jacob was thoroughly impressed by Hacker X, the nickname they had given their rescuer. He was as eager to meet this hacker as Farrell and Victor were.

Neil's arrest had not stopped the hackers from attacking and now they had found a second source of attack. By analyzing the pattern of commands, Farrell established that there were certainly two different groups of hackers involved on that day. A new friend had emerged on the scene.

"Remember this is without Neil," he thought.

Victor had a long and hectic day at the office. He wanted to get home early and headed to the district of Hollis as quickly as the traffic allowed. Despite a detour he was caught in New York's rush hour traffic on Grande Central Parkway. After being stuck there for almost twenty minutes, he turned off the main road. He was near York College which offered a relatively longer but less busy route home. Suddenly he saw a black Chrysler SUV next to his car. He didn't notice it properly until it was too late. The SUV was in front of his car and he had to stop.

This was completely unexpected and although he stopped, his instincts told him that something dangerous was about to happen. His fears proved correct when he saw two masked men emerge from the SUV. Victor was thinking how to escape by reversing his car but one of the men had already reached the driver's door. Both men were armed and now knocked on the car door. Victor's mind worked desperately, trying to find a way to flee.

Reversing the car at high speed and then turning away, they opened fire and Victor was now dodging bullets. He was in the direct line of fire of the two men, one of whom was carrying a small assault rifle, a customized MP5 whilst the other man was holding a 9mm handgun. He assessed how much time it would take for him to change gear and accelerate to flee the bullets. He was not a weapons expert but he considered making this calculation correctly would be a matter of life and death.

Before he could make any move at all, Victor's phone rang.

He was about to ignore it when the person with the 9mm gun signaled him to take the call. To Victor, this was good news in a way because whoever his nemeses were, they at least wanted to talk and maybe make some demands instead of killing him outright.

He took the call reluctantly and when he had finished, had a frightened look on his face. He opened the car door and got out with both hands in the air. One of the masked men grabbed his hands and tied them together behind his back using electrical plastic wire tags. A second later they put a black mask on his head to obscure his vision.

"Move," he heard one of his two kidnappers say.

“Stay quiet and do as we say,” he growled. “Don’t try any nonsense or we’ll harm your family.” The second voice made direct contact with his ear as he spoke and sent a chill down Victor’s spine.

“Take it easy, don’t harm my family. I’ll do whatever you ask.” Victor was now practically pleading with them.

“We’ll see about that when we reach our destination.” said one of the kidnappers.

In the earlier phone call, it had been explained to Victor that his son and wife were already in captivity and if he wanted see them again alive he was to cooperate with his captors. Victor had decided not to annoy them for the safety of his family. He was pushed onto the back seat of the black SUV while one of his captors sat beside him. In just a few minutes the SUV started to move towards its destination. Victor felt a needle inserted in his arm, a sharp cold prick. Within minutes, he was completely unconscious. The last thing he could remember was an image of his wife and son.

***

Elsewhere, Natalie was once again summoned by Fu Wang to meet on an urgent basis. He wanted to expedite their strategy to penetrate the Waverley Davis server network after the latest development which could jeopardize not only their operation but their lives as well.

She informed Jenifer about the call from Fu asking for an emergency meeting and asked her advice for her own security.

Natalie asked Jenifer on the phone. She was in a food market and it was pretty noisy so she could only just hear. “I wonder what the emergency could be,” she asked.

“We can’t talk about it on the phone. Go back to your apartment and let me know when you arrive. I’ll meet you there,” Jenifer answered.

“Ok. I’ll be at my place in about twenty minutes,” Natalie said, looking at her watch. Jenifer confirmed once again that she would be there around the same time.

Within half an hour, they were both looking at monitors in Natalie’s flat. “How can I tell?” Jenifer asked.

“Tell what?” Natalie asked.

“What he wants to meet about,” she said again.

“Come on! You monitor their network twenty-four hours a day. Is anything strange happening? How come you don’t know anything unusual?” Natalie was clearly puzzled.

“I’m certain it has nothing to do with the Waverley Davis server network, most probably they’re going to give you another kind of bug for me to plant on Neil’s mobile,” Jenifer said.

She thought, then said, “You know what. Sometimes, I really feel sorry for this Neil guy. He’ll be in lots of trouble if they find out about this device in his cell phone then he’ll be caught,” Natalie said.

“That’s not our headache. It’s nothing personal against him,” Jenifer said sternly.

“Do you know you sound like a sociopathic character?” Natalie had not liked Jenifer’s remarks about Neil.

Jenifer argued, “Anyway, how long have you started to care about Neil?”

“Care about Neil? What are you saying girl? I’ve just seen pictures of him on my computer which you put there. I don’t know him. It’s not about if I care about him or not. It’s about being human, having feelings. Indifference is the epitome of all evil,” Natalie struck back.

“Natalie! Listen to me. Fools do not survive in this world for too long particularly not in our line of work. A hacker is always a fugitive. We never know when some law officer or intelligence agency will start an investigation even on an old case and begin to find clues leading them to us. Hiding from the world, remaining anonymous is compulsive for this job. It’s not a choice. More relationships mean more vulnerability. Now if you insist, I’ll happily accept that I’m a sociopath and I can live with it without giving a damn about it. But remember to keep in mind, sometimes survival has its price." This time Jenifer kept her tone calmer as she realized that her answers were getting more aggressive.

Natalie took some time to process what Jenifer had just said. She didn't say anything, she didn't want to continue the argument any more but within her mind she was finding it unable to suppress the thought that their actions could lead Neil to being arrested and sent to jail, all because of them.

Little did she know but she was already too late.

"I think it would be better if we both go," Jenifer broke the silence in the room after some time. Natalie nodded her head quietly. "Then it's time to have our insurance policy ready," Jenifer said.

"What do you mean by that?" Natalie asked.

"You'll be wired and your conversation will be recorded on your mobile. Run the voice recorder application as soon as you meet him," she explained before they left to meet Fu Wang at the restaurant. "You'll record all his conversation."

"Won't this implicate me as well?" Natalie showing a little reservation.

"Yes, it can but not if you converse carefully. Don't give lengthy replies. Keep your answers as short as possible and as indirect as you can. Make him talk more. I'm not alone, there are many sociopaths out there and you never know what might unfold tomorrow," Jenifer explained slowly so that Natalie could comprehend everything.

Natalie was staring at Jenifer trying to understand the true nature of her. Jenifer had a soft spot inside her but she would always play tough. Natalie now saw a caring person in the same body where a moment earlier she had seen a complete sociopath.

Both got ready and left to meet Fu Wang completely unaware of the fact that their intense argument had been recorded and listened to some place not far from the apartment. Jenifer had to do extra work concealing herself behind glasses and a wig which transformed her straight blonde hair to curly black. These two small changes made her look very different and it was almost impossible to identify her.

Once they reached the restaurant, they parted ways. Jenifer entered the small restaurant before Natalie and spotted Fu Wang there. She took a table next to him pretending to be a stranger. She sat on a chair with her back towards Fu Wang's back. Natalie came in ten minutes later. She walked up to Fu Wang who demanded to know why she was so late. Natalie just wanted to know what Fu Wang had to tell her and then she wanted to get out of there as soon as possible.

“What’s the emergency?” she asked ignoring Fu Wang’s question.

“Your contact at Waverley Davis has been busted by the FBI.” Fu Wang’s reply shocked Natalie. She could not help but remember her earlier argument with Jenifer about the fate of Neil. She didn’t have a clue what to say. She had even mentioned the FBI. “Ask him about the details.” Suddenly, she heard Jenifer’s voice through a tiny earpiece. This was standard issue in such cases.

“So how did that happen?” Natalie asked Fu Wang.

“The details are not important. We must expedite our operation. An awful lot is on the line including our lives,” Fu Wang replied, making Natalie feel uncomfortable.

“So what you want me to do?” Natalie asked.

“You’ll have to meet and hack someone else just like you did with that idiot who’s now in jail.” He handed over an envelope to Natalie, continuing, “You’ll have to make your move in the next two days.”

Natalie opened the envelope and took out two pictures of two new young men, one of whom was certainly another employee at the Waverley Davis network.

“Payment will be double this time. Here’s your package,” Fu Wang said handing over a package to her. Natalie didn’t like what she found inside that package. There was a mobile phone which had the same malicious codes that Natalie and Jenifer were still analyzing and there was a listening wire which she was to put on while meeting with her next target. Fu Wang ended the meeting. Natalie and Jenifer left the restaurant one-by-one and returned to Natalie's apartment.

"I don't think it's going to end anytime soon and now with this new demand of putting a wire on me, I've started to feel this game is more dangerous than I'd thought. Worse, we know Neil's in jail because of us. Remember that Neil knows nothing about Natalie, so we can't implicate her."

"Relax, we can get out of this with no connection but we'll have to remain focused and careful. Panicking won't help at all," Jenifer said.

"We can still get out of this? I think I did give you a solution for that but you wanted to stay involved." Natalie was now furious at Jenifer for rejecting her proposal of vanishing and not coming back to New York.

"Yes, you did and I accept that I screwed it up for both of us by rejecting the idea at the time," Jenifer said.

"We need to act fast and think of some kind of a solution. We must be prepared to disappear in case things go wrong." Natalie was still considering fleeing from New

York as a safety strategy. On the other hand, Jenifer had very different plans.

“No need to do that. Neil is the only one who’s seen my face. Now he’s in jail that’s good news. It makes it easier for you to impersonate me. You can now meet your new target freely. By the way who is he?”

“I don’t know. Here’s his photo.” Natalie handed over the envelope to Jenifer.

“He looks like a tech nerd,” she said.

“Who is he?”

“His name’s Farrell Miller, he’s on the security team.”

“I want you to be there with me when we meet just like you were today,” Natalie said.

Jenifer nodded her head, “Yes, no problem.”

***

Christopher’s voice crackled on the two way radio as he addressed all the squad members. “All units are in place, the targets have arrived and there is a positive identification. Only proceed on my command, over.”

“Remember rescuing hostages is our primary goal in this operation. No discharging weapons unless there is a life threatening situation and then only on my command. Is that clear? Over and out." He put down his radio.

Under his command were four different FBI S.W.A.T teams. They had already been deployed to encircle the warehouse. This was where Fu Wang conducted his operations. Just then a large black SUV entered the warehouse lot carrying Victor. His son and wife were already there.

Lee had orchestrated these kidnappings.

It seemed that Victor was the last member of his family to be taken. Two teams of professional kidnappers had been used to track and pick Victor's family up.

Victor's wife and son had been taken inside the warehouse. FBI agents, hiding at various places nearby, were taking photos to ascertain that Victor had also been brought there. Once confirmed, the entire squad waited for the final order to storm the warehouse. Christopher wanted to ensure that all the victims were safe before giving a final green light to his team.

The order from Christopher came within a few minutes and the FBI's hostage recovery squad began to move in. Sharpshooters took care of two men on the top floor of the warehouse. Two guards were stationed outside the main gate. They were taken out by silent weapons.

The warehouse was divided into many areas by six foot high vinyl partitioning walls. The light levels inside the warehouse were extremely dim as such it was not an ideal place for intense close quarter combat offering as it did many places to hide and out maneuver each other.

This portion of the warehouse in particular was not the perfect place to carry out the impending raid because, prior to the raid, it had had a slightly different floor plan layout with fewer partition divisions. Now, the new layout changed the situation and forced the FBI squad to reassess the situation once again. They had just a few minutes to make a decision. With the elimination of the four guards, retreating and planning the rescue mission again was not now an option.

They had to push on regardless so, tactically, the squad was advised to use low light. Inside the compound, the lower light levels gave them the advantage of conducting a sweep without engaging any of the captors and enabled them to find the exact location of the hostages inside.

Trying this tactic out in a practice raid would normally be compulsory in order to improve the chances of the rescue operation being more successful. The two teams each entered into the warehouse to search for the hostages and assess the best possible way for their safe extraction. The clock was ticking and time was running out. The plan was that they should extract the hostages and then they should exit the building.

Instead, after fifteen intense minutes, the first team broke the silence and informed operation command about the location and condition of the hostages. There were twelve men inside the warehouse as well as two others in an adjacent office. One of those in the office was Lee.

The four men inside the compound were ordered to take positions to protect the hostages whilst a further team of ten was to escort the hostages to safety and eliminate anyone who tried to resist. Two advanced teams had already helped tactical support to draw an accurate schematic sketch of the partitioning and a safe passage through the tactical maze.

Thankfully, the operation was completed in less than twenty minutes. Victor and his family were safe. Two FBI operatives were wounded in the ensuing gun battle. The Chinese tried to resist but, with the help of the tactical support team's skilled input, the FBI squad was able to overcome and eliminate them without too much trouble.

Lee was amongst the dead.

The squad finished a sweep of the warehouse to gather all the evidence and collect the dead bodies. They had no idea of the treasure trove inside the lower basement.

***

Natalie was walking back and forth restlessly in her apartment thinking about Neil's arrest and the possible outcome of any FBI investigation. She was scared and wanted to leave New York but Jenifer still rejected her alternative plan. She was not able to find Fu Wang or his group on their dark net hackers' forum either. This was almost unheard of. It looked like they had gone to ground.

She was thinking about the time when she and Jenifer had had their heated argument. She tried to make sense of Jenifer's exit plan. How long would it take the Chinese to figure out that the real reason behind the continuing failure of their cyber-attacks on the Waverley Davis network security was down to Jenifer? How would they react to it?

"Too many questions, and not many answers," she thought.

She called Jenifer and told her about the new situation. Jenifer set off in her car to continue the conversation at Natalie's apartment.

"So what do you think about the future line of action now?" Natalie asked.

"Slow down Natalie, nothing is going to happen to us, there's no way they can trace any of this back to us."

"How long do think the FBI would take to find that second bug on his mobile?" Natalie asked.

"They should already have found it by now, I think," answered Jenifer.

Natalie once again asked the important question, "Don't you think they would also have found your name in his contact list?" She stopped talking when she saw Jenifer was grinning.

"See, I told you. Nothing is going to happen that soon. All the FBI can do is to try to trace the number of some girl named Clarke and they won't be able to because I dumped the phone I used and destroyed the SIM."

It took a while but the stress etched on Natalie's face began to disappear. Natalie grabbed Jenifer in her arms and pulled her towards her as if Jenifer had saved Natalie from the grip of some unseen phantom.

"Now let's focus on the work at hand. Tell me, when you are going to make a move on Farrell and what will be your approach?" she asked Natalie.

Unknown to them both, this conversation was going to make their lives really complicated in the coming days. Both girls were unaware of the bug under Natalie's table which was transmitting the entire conversation to a warehouse building where, at that very moment, the Chinese were listening, or at least they would have been, if the building was not right now being raided by the FBI cyber division.

Chapter Nine

"You willed yourself to where you are today, so will yourself out of it."

Stephen Richards

Neil was still in FBI custody where he had begun to reflect on the events that had led to his current predicament. Over the last few days he had tried to think about every possible scenario in which his mobile had been left unprotected and therefore compromised. He remembered that, other than software updates to his Android mobile OS, he had not downloaded anything for at least the last sixty days. Then he tried to recall events and places where he had been but once again he was unable to remember a single moment when he had left his mobile unattended.

"How the hell was my mobile hacked?" Finding the answer to this question had become the most important task for him right now but he still had no idea. He wondered whether his parents had been told about his arrest or not. He hoped and prayed that they would never have to know.

Neil was grilled very aggressively by the FBI during the first few days after his arrest. He was interviewed multiple times by different people including crime specialists, cyber security specialists, psychiatrists and communication specialists. He understood that he was being probed from different angles. No one from Waverley Davis had contacted him since his arrest. He was detained in a loose wired kind of small chamber with no windows, only a small air inlet to keep the fresh air flowing in and a dim light. He could not even hear any outside noises. This was like solitary confinement and it began to wreak havoc on his nerves. He was not charged or even given access to a lawyer and this seemed to indicate the fact that he was to be charged with treason or some other anti-state allegations. The FBI was using intense psychological tactics to break his will but Neil was no criminal.

He was also aware that the punishment for treason was the death penalty.

With every passing day, Neil found it increasingly difficult to keep his sanity intact. He fought inner demons, fear and despondency, when each crept into his thoughts like vultures. An intense feeling of people trying to break his will stared him in the eyes and Neil desperately tried to push this feeling of hopelessness away by thinking about and visualizing his early release from custody.

The Law of Attraction focuses on what you want to achieve. He thought of what he wanted and not give any thought to what he did not want.

Your subconscious mind only hears the thing being asked for so, in a request to be free from prison, your mind only hears 'being in prison' and that is exactly what has happened here he thought. He had learnt this art of visualization from Ajay, by listening to his motivational talks when he delivered them during conferences and on his travels to many lectures abroad.

In these dire circumstances, Neil decided to use the universal Law of Attraction. Suddenly a ray of light illuminated his thoughts and now he imagined being free. But a mere wish or craving for freedom was not going to get him out of this crisis. He knew he must not lose hope at that time.

Initially, the shock of his sudden arrest and the dim and spine-chilling environment of his cell pushed him towards an abyss of hopelessness. Now this sudden ray of light was helping him to crawl away from that psychological pit. What at first had seemed impossible was now very possible in his subconscious. He was to start right now. He had to defeat the thought that freedom was far from impossible. He had to make it possible; firstly in his mind and then in reality. He closed his eyes and took a trip down memory lane within his brain.

Stop using words like impossible only possible, negative thoughts beget more negative thoughts.

"Everything is impossible until it becomes possible."

Finally, Neil recalled something Ajay had told him a long time ago.

"Nothing is impossible even the word impossible itself announces that 'I AM possible'. Neil heard Ajay once again. He remembered that this was the most fascinating sentence he had heard in a conference and it had made a lasting impression.

The possibility began to be created in his own mind. By just thinking about his freedom, things had already begun to move in that direction. Meanwhile the FBI had discovered lots of items from inside the warehouse where Victor and his family had been recovered from. One of the items was a curious device with a delicate transmit and receive functionality. Spiritually, things were still moving in his favor. Yet, unbeknown to Neil, it was still going to take a long time before he would attain his freedom.

Little did he know that his predicament was going to get a lot more calamitous before his imagined recovery became a reality; a potential darkness before the dawn.

***

The operation by the FBI was almost concluded. “Did you find anything from the basement?” Christopher asked James, one of his squad members, who had led the operation to recover Victor and his family from captivity. “Yes, lots,” he replied. “Lots of computer parts like hard drives, RAM chips and some unknown gadget.”

“The recovered items are with forensics,” James reported

“What about the unknown gadget? Christopher asked. “What’s the unknown gadget then?

"I've absolutely no idea. Even forensics found it a complete mystery. We're still checking."

"OK. I'll get more information when I talk to forensics. Have we any news on the identity of the dead captors yet?" Christopher asked.

"Yes sir. One of them has been identified as a North Korean citizen who came to the US a few weeks ago on a tourist visa," James replied.

"North Korean origin…. are you positive?" Christopher asked with astonishment.

"Yes sir. Immigration confirmed it after checking his profile matching. He was clearly identified."

"What about the rest of these guys?" Christopher asked.

"Mostly locals, with ethnic Asian backgrounds; a couple of them are wanted in multiple homicides and some petty crimes."

"Thanks, James," said Christopher and then asked him to leave. He picked up the phone and dialed Kerstin Miles, the chief forensic investigation officer with the FBI. "What did you made of that mysterious device we recovered?"

"Well, Christopher, this device contains a memory unit as well. The strange thing is that it's small, not more than a few gigabytes but even that is space enough to hold basic information. We don't want to harm it anyway."

"So, what data did you recover?" he asked.

"So far nothing because the drive is heavily encrypted," Kerstin explained.

"How long it is going to take before you crack the encryption?" he asked.

"Can't say for sure, but you can definitely say one thing with certainty, this is a highly sophisticated device which also has the ability to transmit and receive and that is still active on this unit," she explained.

"Then we must go after the signal it's sending and receiving," he said with excitement in his voice.

"Yes. That would certainly lead us to some solid proof. We're trying to isolate the communication chip that transmits and receives from the memory unit so that we can work on both things in tandem. You'll be the first to know as soon as soon we get that done," she replied.

"What about the other hard drives recovered?" Christopher asked.

"They're encrypted too and we've already sent a request to NASA research department to help us decipher the content. Unfortunately all our resources here have been tightly squeezed," she explained.

“So it’s all about waiting and been patient then,” Christopher said and put the phone down.

***

Natalie was still trying to find Fu Wang on various dark net forums, the most common sites used by hacker forums that she could access. “Nothing. He’s vanished.” Natalie was amazed by the sudden disappearance of Fu Wang. These dark net forums were their only way to communicate. Tunneling Tor forums meant it was nearly impossible to be traced. Hackers all over the world used them to exchange ideas freely. Jenifer and Natalie were also among the hundreds of thousands of regular users.

“Well, what exactly is TOR?” Jenifer asked.

“Well, it was originally developed with the US Navy in mind mainly for the purpose of protecting government communications. Today, it’s used every day for a wide variety of purposes by the military, journalists, law enforcement officers, activists and mostly hackers,” answered Natalie.

They had also asked many mutual friends about Fu Wang but no one had a clue about him. Natalie wanted to tell Fu Wang about her meeting with Farrell which had gone well but Natalie had been unable to bug his phone because Farrell had had to leave urgently after receiving a call from his office. The fact they could not contact Fu Wang on any of the TOR forums left both Jenifer and Natalie trying to understand the possible reason for his sudden disappearance.

Jenifer was thinking about ways she could contact the mysterious person whose one mobile cell phone call had instigated this entire Waverley Davis cyber-attack episode. That person had told her to connect to Fu Wang and then, after that one initial call, had not contacted her again. Fu Wang had told her that all her business would now be conducted through him. He would be the one giving her assignments and taking feedback. She was paid well so at the time she had decided not to take any interest in the other people working within Fu Wang's organization. This presented a problem and seemed to be a bad omen to Jenifer. She had not yet been paid for the second bug implant which she was promised would be a higher than the payment for her first task. The second mission, to hack Neil's mobile, was complete and she should at least have been paid. Now, all her hopes of continuing this lucrative money stream were fading fast.

She had kept most of her earnings as savings but, with her mother's treatment at an expensive private clinic, draining her resources, her funds were quickly depleting. She had to act fast in order to get back in contact with the Chinese urgently.

"What do we do if he's been arrested?" Natalie asked.

“That’s highly unlikely because if that’s the case we both would have been arrested by now too. This is something else. Pretty damn serious,” Jenifer reasoned as an answer.

“OK. But how else can you explain his sudden disappearance?” Natalie asked.

“I’ve no logical answer to that right now but things should become clearer in a couple of hours,” Jenifer thought. She was trying to keep calm herself but she knew that Fu Wang would not ever voluntarily disappear on a live mission especially during a security operation.

This was national operational protocol.

Jenifer was worried about her mother’s treatment but at the same time was also engrossed in finding Fu Wang online. She started to scan the network in the hope of finding any clue about Fu Wang or his team but drew a complete blank on this mission. Now she had also begun to think about the possibility of Fu Wang being in the FBI’s custody. If this was true, this was really bad news for her considering her dependence on being paid for this contract.

“We’re going to own them,” Jenifer said after thinking for few minutes.

“Own who?” Natalie asked.

"Their entire network," Jenifer answered. "The Chinese will be flushed out of the Waverley Davis system and we won't bug Farrell," she added. Natalie was trying to make sense of the gibberish coming from Jenifer's mouth.

"OK. Then just two questions. How and Why?"

"I know their vulnerabilities. Even though they have considerably hardened their network, I can still sneak in undetected and because I need the money for keeping Mom in that expensive clinic and to pay the rest of my bills including the rent on that apartment of yours."

"We can cover that doing other projects," Natalie said. She could write programming modules for various online clients. She had been earning good money through this source before Jenifer had told her to stop that work and be her partner in this new game of industrial espionage.

"Natalie you must understand that we need more than that." Jenifer said. Natalie was quiet because she knew that Jenifer was right. They needed the extra money for taking care of Jenifer's mother whose condition had been worsening despite all the necessary medication and care the home could provide to counteract the aging process that compounded the paralysis of Jenifer's mother.

"OK, what's the plan?" Natalie asked.

"The plan, my dear, is to get into that network, open a backdoor and sell that information for the best price. Will you be OK with that? We don't know what we'll be handing over or who to but who cares as long as we get paid," she added.

Natalie's humane side persisted.

"Morality, judgment, good and evil, the existence of God, faith and divine punishments. All these things are areas of the world I don't give a thought to," Jenifer said. "Maybe you're right, I am in all respects a sociopath after all, or fast becoming one. That's been my conditioning since I was able to reason, Natalie, I can't help it. That's just the way I am, there's no other way." Jenifer's reply stunned Natalie. Usually, Jenifer had a habit of arguing with Natalie but not this time, she had finally conceded defeat on this point.

"If we're to take control of their network, we need someone from inside Waverley Davis. We'll need to rewrite our own malware to take control. We can't get into their internal network because even you haven't been successful in penetrating that. So how are we going to achieve it?" Natalie asked.

"Through the only way possible now Neil is no longer our access route and that's to somehow get Jacob, the son of Ajay Mohan, to work with us knowingly or otherwise at Waverley Davis. Until very recently Ajay just happened to be the biggest inspiration in my life," Jenifer boasted.

"That must mean you were already working on that plan," Natalie said in amazement.

"No," Jenifer replied, "when the Chinese were using my services and things were OK with them, it just became a curiosity really. That changed slightly when Neil got arrested. And then the plan to use Jacob became a realistic possibility, more so than ever now because of Fu Wang's sudden disappearance. All of a sudden, this has to become our primary plan and we don't have a choice. With that in mind I've been following him closely and can easily find a way to make contact with him if need be," Jenifer told her friend.

"You didn't respond to the last part of my question." Natalie wanted to know why Jenifer chose to work against Waverley Davis when Ajay Mohan was once her inspiration in life.

"That's because my inspirations were shot down by my circumstances and my choices. I could have gone straight to Waverley Davis and informed them about the Chinese episode but choose not to. With my expertise I might have even found a job there as well," Jenifer replied.

"So what do we do with my mission with Farrell now? Should, we continue or stop the whole thing?"

Jenifer digressed slightly, "Teresa! Did you like him? I mean Farrell," she asked. This was a surprise, she had used her real name and Natalie knew whenever Jenifer did that, it was to indicate that she was giving her an honest reply.

"I was focused on my job. I never gave Farrell a single thought and in any event the meeting was too brief," Jenifer sighed as part of her answer.

"But, being honest," Natalie made a confession, "I wish I was able to forget the fact that someone was behind bars because of us." This was her way of an apology.

"Thanks and let's drop your assignment. We're not going to work for the Chinese anymore," Jenifer said in decisive tone. She was furious that the Chinese had not paid her for her last assignment which she had completed for them successfully. Natalie was relieved to learn that at least now, whatever they would both be doing, she would know all about it.

***

Ajay had asked Victor to stay at home with his family to recuperate after the kidnap for as long as he or his family wanted to. It was obvious to Victor that the captivity of his family and the cyber-attacks were directly linked. The FBI had explained the connection after completing the mission to recover Victor and his family.

Jacob was pleased that Victor and his family were safe. He was also glad to have his technical genius back by his side to resume their fight to protect Waverley Davis and the besieged cyber fortress. Victor rejoined the office just three days after his release. However, Jacob had remained in a constant state of shock during the entire period of Victor's kidnapping. He thought about doing other aspects of his job to break his routine and disconnect from the digital world of Waverley Davis. Now that Victor was back, he could do this.

One day shortly afterwards, Jacob found himself walking around an art exhibition in a well-known art gallery in New York. He was enjoying the people more than the art if he was honest and it was good to see a gathering like this where every face was smiling, cheerful and no-one wore a single sign of worry. The environment of the gallery affected Jacob's mood too. He began to feel fresh, almost alive again. He was very conscious about this change of feeling. Suddenly, he realized that every now and again he would remember Ajay telling him that, to keep ourselves mindful, we must break our daily life circle. He had done that today and smiled when he realized how true Ajay's advice was.

"So much art here to enjoy and still people get lost. Isn't it unfortunate?" he heard a female voice say.

In an instant, Jacob was back in the room conscious of his presence in the gallery and listening to that soft voice. He looked to his right from where the voice had come from and there she was; a beautiful blonde girl in black attire smiling and looking back at Jacob who remained perplexed by the whole situation.

“You weren’t here. Were you?” she asked before Jacob could say anything.

“Excuse me?” Jacob said with eyes wide open.

The pretty girl blushed for a moment or so “What’s the point of coming here if you’re still someplace else in your thoughts?” she asked.

“How long had she been watching me thinking about Dad?” he thought.

“I think you saw something which made you think and smile,” the girl said looking at Jacob.

“Yes, you’re right I guess,” Jacob said.

“So who were you thinking about, must be someone very special,” the girl asked whilst gazing intently at Jacob’s face.

“Yeah, my Dad,” he said smiling again and then he noticed that the girl clearly was not expecting that answer.

“Unusual and unexpected,” she said. “Must be a special dad,” she added.

“He’s very special,” Jacob replied, with the warm glow in his eyes clearly indicating the close bond he felt with his father.

“That’s great. Not everyone’s fond of their fathers or perhaps not all people are born to great dads,” she said with a slight hint at an unhappy time in her past remembered. Jacob was intrigued by her strange answer. “So you enjoy art exhibitions regularly?” she asked as she continued the small talk.

“No, just trying to disconnect myself from the daily cycle of normal life.” he replied. He continued “I was just passing the museums when I stumbled upon this place. And you?” he added quickly.

“I try to enjoy the efforts of artistic minds whenever I can find free time,” she told him. “Work keeps me busy but we all need food for our aesthetic minds,” she added.

“I don’t know how abstract art like this can help with that?!” Jacob said.

“Well, in my opinion, art is much more than what first meets the eye. It’s a reflection of the thoughts of the artist. First he dreams his painting and then paints his dream,” she said while looking at a small piece of art on the wall in front of them. Jacob had started to find her interesting.

Now they were looking at a bigger painting in which the artist had used long strokes in darker colours. “Intensity;

this is what the artist was feeling in his mind when he was painting it," she commented.

"How do you know what was in his mind?" he asked.

"His thoughts are there in the art," she said laughing.

"There is a famous proverb that art should disturb the comfortable and comfort the disturbed. That's exactly what the artist achieved here," she commented on another piece where dark shaded colours were used in the middle while the outer region of the painting had a lighter tone. The internal colours were stroked in such a way that each colour collided with the other while lighter colours on the edges spread outwards as if they were trying to escape the canvas.

Jacob was impressed by her comments as he was finding that exact feeling of discomfort looking at the painting. It was too late, Jacob was fascinated by her.

"You know art also plays a big role in creating whatever mankind invents, it was developed once as a piece of art. That's why any sophisticated invention in science is known as state of art technology," she explained

Jacob had never imagined art like this. He did not know he was speaking to Jenifer.

"Thoughts become things," said Jenifer, quoting a proverb from the deity Buddha. "Your thoughts become reality, just by thinking about them," Jenifer said even louder this time.

"How can they?" he asked.

"It's simple. Whenever our mind has a thought that it would like to become reality, it visualizes it as real then and, most importantly, only then, your mind believes it can make manifest by bringing about the creation of those thoughts," Jenifer said with a smile on her face.

"That contradicts all the amazing achievements in science, culture and the arts. Their creation demanded much more than that." Jacob's subconscious had taken control. Just thinking about something and wishing it would happen was never going to get any results in practical life. His reality thought process had taken over his conscious mind and was dictating this conversation.

"I'm Jenifer," the girl introduced herself with her hand extended towards him.

"Pleased to meet you, I'm Jacob," he replied, shaking hands with her. Both looked into each other's eyes. They chatted away and Jacob found it amazing that Jenifer had similar preferences in music, food, movies and travel, almost identical to his. They chatted a little longer and on departure exchanged numbers and promised to catch up with each other some other time soon.

***

Neil focused on the word impossible to associate with his dismal circumstances and then he visualized ways to negate those circumstances. Neil was practically attracting his freedom or at least that was what he was trying to do. “Impossible is just a big word thrown around by small men who find it easier to live in the world they’ve been given than to explore the power they have to change it. Impossible is not a fact. It’s an opinion. Impossible is not a declaration. It’s a dare. Impossible is potential. Impossible is temporary. Impossible is nothing,” he recalled the words of great Muhammad Ali.

“My detention is temporary….” Ali stated, “And the Truth shall be revealed and I shall be out soon.” He was so confident that he went on to assure his friends that, “This is my will.” Mysteriously, history records the fact that the great Muhammad Ali would only serve half of his draft violation sentence of two years.

Being jailed for draft evasion at that time in the 1960s in a white dominated judicial system in America meant his chances of overturning a court’s decision were virtually nil. The Law of Attraction proved to be present in this instance. Because no legal decision was made, Mohammed Ali never knew or understood how he won his case except for a compromise proposed by Justice Stewart, the trail judge, stating that “Ali’s conviction would be reversed citing a technical error by the Justice Department.” Ali gradually won unanimous assent from the eight voting justices. Still, this case remains a complete mystery today. Neil had visualized walking out of custody suite with his head held high and with the FBI agents apologizing for his detention. "I must act now to make this happen sooner rather than later," he thought. He started to recall the events of the previous few weeks. He began to remember his days at Waverley Davis and the memories occupied his time. He pictured his daily routine in the office, speaking to Ajay, time spent with Jacob his friends, colleagues and work mates. Then one particular face popped up into his memory. It was Clarke, he really remembered her the most.

"She must be really worried about me and my sudden disappearance," Neil thought.

Recalling their last date, he put the memories into slow motion in order to pick up anything suspicious that he could have missed. As soon as he imagined Clarke taking her photo, his eyes opened wide. His rational mind tried to process the scenario to draw a final conclusion.

Then he recalled the moment when he left his mobile in her hands. But that was to take some fun pictures so what possible motive could she have had to do something like this to me? Yet she could have infected the phone, she had the opportunity. Neil was perplexed.

He processed the facts about Clarke once again but again failed to find a motive. "What if she was working with the hacking group all that time?" he thought. "No. She can't be," he answered himself. "Let's face it," he mumbled, "she didn't mention any knowledge of computers or anything technical in all the time we went out." Then he thought, "Really, he had no information about Clarke at all."

She had never given him clear answers to any of his questions about her life. She would always change the topic in such a way that Neil had to keep talking. Sometimes she would talk about philosophical things in life, such as the subconscious mind, human behavior and karma, other spiritual things. She never told him anything about her personal life other than that she was born into a middle class white family. When she was younger her father had passed away and the sad fact was that now her mother was confined to a wheelchair. Neil had no idea where she lived or what she actually did or who her friends were. On the other hand, Neil was like an open book to her. She knew almost everything about him other than the details of his work life. However this did not make her guilty and responsible for his detention.

Neil had to force this train of thought about Clarke out of his head because there was just no proof. He was again suffering with depression and this time it was really bad.

Chapter Ten

"The starting point of all achievement is DESIRE. Keep this constantly in mind. Weak desire brings weak results, just as a small fire makes a small amount of heat."

Napoleon Hill

It was a tough period in time for Ping May, the senior Chinese chief intelligence officer because his operation to secure or destroy the secret US Navy cyber weapon had failed miserably. Not only had he failed to achieve the mission's objective, he had also lost one of his finest hit man. He was enraged but that day he was in a meeting convened to undertake a critical appraisal of Ping May's plan and execution strategy. The meeting was taking place in the Chinese intelligence headquarters where senior leaders of the country's Pollitt Bureau members including Li Jingling and the top military leadership or their representatives were attending.

Firstly, I would like to brief all the honorable members of the meeting about our primary mission in the US. It was learned by Chinese Naval intelligence eight months ago that one of the leading US military contractors had been awarded a top secret project for the US Navy. Waverley Davis, the military contractor, is one of a kind within the American military industrial complex. We couldn't find out what this weapon actually was. Was it new hardware, or a new cyber weapon? Nothing was sure except the fact that this new system or weapon was somehow related to the latest generation of military satellites on which all seven fleets of the US Navy depend for their navigation and operations. Our cyber dark army launched a two stage exploitation and attack after successfully hacking into the mobile phone of one of the Waverley Davis employees.

We were able to partially see their internal network without being detected.

Somehow, Waverley Davis was able to thwart our cyber efforts. Their defense strategy strengthened after our successive failures. The person responsible for Waverley Davis' security was abducted by our assets in the US. Our asset was working undercover as a North Korean tourist. The plan was to extract information about various authentication credentials from him. However, the FBI became aware of our plan in advance and raided the warehouse where the captive and his family were being kept hostage. Subsequently, we lost one our biggest assets along with all his local team of agents. The result was that the hostage and his family were recovered by the FBI. This created a serious crisis for China because the same warehouse was being used by our dark army team who had left many of the mission's secret devices behind before moving to another safe house out of town.

As soon as we knew that the FBI was closing in on our dark operations team it was eliminated by our permanent agents working in the USA with diplomatic immunity as there was no time for their safe exfiltration. Basically, we cleansed our own operation by sabotage. This act was compulsory, not from choice. To prevent the FBI from recovering the data from the devices and items left in the warehouse, our team implanted fictitious hardware drives on the units. These contained loaded Nano-scale

Electronic Magnetic Plate weapons. These should cripple the electronic circuitry of any US system apart from them then begin to self-destruct. We may have lost a battle in the US but we are not going to lose the war.

"I consider myself responsible for the failure of our project and the loss of the lives of Chinese dark army members and present my resignation as Chief of Intelligence. I will accept every decision of the Chinese government, Communist party and Pollitt Bureau," said Ping May describing the details of Chinese operation in the US and accepting his failure as the Chinese spy chief. His resignation was accepted by the Chinese leadership. A new spy chief was appointed who was tasked to devise a new strategy to complete the main goal.

***

After a long time, Victor and Farrell began to relax, the cyber threats had vanished. Victor kept thinking about his abduction while Farrell's mind was occupied by the thought of Neil and his role in the cyber-attacks and his eventual arrest.

"Do you believe Neil was involved?" Farrell asked.

"Not for one second," Victor replied.

"Why?"

"Because that's what my instinct tells me and, he's not been charged so far. I'm certain the FBI couldn't find any further connection to him in these attacks," Victor explained.

"Then what about his bugged mobile, how would you explain that?" Farrell asked.

"Well, that's because smart phones are like computers. They work online a lot and as such are prone to hacking just like computers. That's their Achilles heel or down side. I'm certain his mobile was hacked," Victor said.

"Hey! Have you seen Jacob lately?" he asked Farrell.

"No, I haven't seen him since yesterday."

Jacob was with Jenifer at that exact moment. Now the cyber issues were resolved, Jacob had found free time to be with this girl who he found really interesting. He remained unable to describe his feelings when he was with her but whatever they were, he wanted the feelings to continue. After a few more dates he would find excuses to meet Jenifer who sometimes said she was unable to meet for a variety of reasons.

That day they were meeting after a week and Jacob was really excited to see Jenifer who was in same black dress she had worn on their first encounter at the art gallery many weeks ago. "You look really great in that dress,"

Jacob said as soon as his gaze fell on Jenifer's slim curved figure.

"That's exactly why I'm in this dress." Jenifer's spontaneous response left Jacob speechless with a smile on his face. Jenifer laughed looking directly into Jacob's face. They had a beautiful meal together that evening in a candle lit restaurant. All evening Jacob wanted to tell Jenifer the strange feelings he felt when he was with her. But unfortunately he couldn't find the right words at the right moment. He would never have imagined he would have trouble expressing himself to Jenifer.

"The food was delicious but I think I enjoyed your company even more." Yes, Finally Jacob had mustered up the courage to express his feelings. Jenifer just smiled and that gave Jacob a little more courage.

"Do you know what I like most about you?" Jacob asked. Jenifer waited. "Your eyes," he continued, "I love the way the light shines off those beautiful blue eyes." Jenifer listened to his compliment and waited to hear more but no more came.

"Thanks for those lovely words," she replied as her bright smile lit her eyes after hearing Jacob's remarks. "Time goes so quickly, in fact it seems to fly whenever we're together," Jenifer said checking her watch.

"Yes, it sure does," he answered and with that, Jacob understood that the date was now nearly over and they would soon have to leave. He felt somehow that Jenifer was trying to return his feelings but for some reason was unable to do so. In reality he was actually right. Jenifer was fighting an internal battle between her heart and her thoughts and it was tearing her apart.

Jacob was thinking of telling Ajay about his feelings for Jenifer but was not sure exactly when to say anything because he had not yet sensed a clear signal from Jenifer that made that communication possible. He was aware that he had not yet spoken those three magical words to her either. "Probably that's what she's waiting for me to say," he hoped. She had, in fact, said nothing in that respect either.

Ajay sat alone in his office at Waverley Davis thinking about his son's behavior. He had noticed that his son's demeanor and distracted attitude was obvious from the way Jacob conducted himself. Many times recently he had noticed that Jacob was not attentive to the moment as if he was not consciously there. In the beginning, Ajay ignored this but Jacob's change of behavior was becoming more and more apparent with each passing day. Ajay realized it was time to talk to his son man to man.

Ajay summoned Jacob into his office. "What's going on with you?" he asked.

"With me? Well, nothing, Dad, I'm just fine." Jacob replied, confused, yet he had pretty good idea what Ajay actually wanted to know. He also wanted to discuss this matter with his father but he was not expecting to have the conversation in the office like this.

"Funnily enough, Dad, there is something I want to talk about with you as well. I think home would be a better place for such discussions, don't you?" Jacob said after thinking for few moments.

Later that evening they continued their conversation. "What's her name?" Ajay asked.

"How do you know it's a girl?" he replied.

"Well you've not been paying much attention since Victor's return. I've noticed recently you're someplace else in your head when we're in in meetings. It's so obvious that you're hanging between some certainty and something totally uncertain. You, my son, are waiting for an answer. So I ask again, what's her name?"

"Jenifer. Her name is Jenifer," Jacob uttered the name of girl who now had his heart.

"Tell me more about her," Ajay added.

"Well, she's attractive, highly intelligent and amazingly beautiful…." Jacob said.

He had not finished his list of compliments before Ajay interrupted, “You forgot charming and gorgeous. Oh Romeo, where for art thou,” he joked. “Sorry, Son, I didn’t mean to mock you,” he added. “I don’t blame you if you’re struggling to express your feelings. Like father, like son,” he thought.

“I was like you in too those early days when I met your mother and I felt something for the first time in my life,” he said. Jacob could see that his father was visualizing moments from his past. “Son, always include me in those things where you feel the most vulnerable so that I can give you some friendly advice,” Ajay added, getting up from his chair. “My only honest advice is always just remember, whatever you say, just make sure that it comes straight from your heart.” He concluded by adding, “That’s what will make it genuine and will help you to attract the people in your life who you really need.”

***

The minute Jenifer set foot in Natalie’s apartment, she heard Natalie say, “Have you seen this?” pointing at the TV where the local newscaster was telling viewers about a raid by the FBI on a building not far from Natalie’s apartment. FBI operatives had recovered five dead bodies including Fu Wang’s. The report told them that all the deceased were killed from close range weapon combat. The FBI had recovered a large cache of digital equipment from the building including computers, laptops, mobile, external storage devices and hard drives. Jenifer eyes were glued to the TV screen while her mind analyzed the possible scenarios which both of them could now face.

She started to assess the potential risks her plan could face in the coming days.

“I think it’s time. We must leave here very soon, it’s no longer safe,” Natalie said almost hysterically. The report on the TV screen was far too overwhelming for her.

“Yes, this time you’re right. All my fears about the danger of working with the Chinese have been proved right today. I think for now you should move to my place and we need to both keep a really low profile.”

“We need to keep a low profile both online and offline if we’re going to escape danger,” Natalie said.

“We should look at this as a positive,” Jenifer said.

“How can any of this possibly be good?” Natalie asked, pointing towards the TV.

“It is good, in that Fu Wang was the only one who knew your face. That means, my friend, he’s the only person who could possibly say that you are Jenifer the hacker. Now he’s dead, that information has gone with him too,” Jenifer explained and Natalie could not disagree.

“I can understand that,” she replied.

“It’s pretty straightforward really,” replied Jenifer “It’s bad because we’ve no idea how much information was recorded about our operation on those computers and laptops that the FBI has recovered. Unfortunately, we’ve not got a clue how much the FBI will know about us in, say, the next two weeks,” Jenifer said.

“For now, at least, we’re in grave danger.” Jenifer looked at Natalie’s face for a few moments then then suddenly took her cell phone from her pocket and smashed it under the heel of her shoe.

Destroying the cell phone and SIM card, she shouted “Grab everything; we’re going to leave here right now. Don’t leave anything behind, not even a toothbrush. Make sure you take everything with you. You can put the rest of the things in some garbage bags, not in the dumpster. When we leave we can burn them or throw them in the Hudson River at the corner of the block. Whatever happens, don’t forget to rub everything clean of any evidence of us having been here.” Jenifer bossed these instructions to Natalie and walked towards the door.

“Where are you going?” Natalie asked.

“I am going to take care of a couple of things to help our survival. You mustn’t worry. I’ll be back in a couple of hours and then I’ll help to clean the place of prints and DNA etc. Start packing first,” Jenifer said as she left Natalie’s apartment. Once outside, she looked carefully down the empty corridor; her sixth sense had warned her about some sort of threat lurking around Natalie's place. Suddenly, she had a strong feeling that in order to keep herself and Natalie safe she would have to execute the radical exit plan she had in mind. Her hands gripped the steering wheel of her car as she drove to meet one of her old acquaintances.

She thought, rather smugly, desperate circumstances call for desperate measures.

***

Neil was charged by the FBI with various cybercrimes against the state including espionage. All of the charges carried Felony One status for potential enemies of the state or non-state actors. According to the penal code on the treason print out which was handed to Neil to read, if any person or persons, owing allegiance to the United States of America, shall levy war against them, or shall adhere to their enemies, giving them aid and comfort within the United States, or elsewhere, and shall be thereof convicted on confession in open court, or on the testimony of two witnesses to the same overt act of the treason whereof he or they shall stand indicted, such person or persons shall be adjudged guilty of treason against the United States, and shall suffer death.

These serious charges of treason were nothing less than a cataclysmic shock for Neil. He could not believe that this was actually happening to him. The tiniest bit of good news in this whole drama for Neil was that he had finally been given access to a lawyer who had visited Neil in jail and at least heard his side of the story.

Neil told him the same things he had already repeatedly told the FBI investigators. Ajay was also shocked when he knew about the exact charges. Everything on that charge sheet contradicted how Ajay perceived Neil to be in his mind's eye. He rejected the charges against Neil but still wanted to know the truth behind the attacks. Neil also faced state espionage charges pressed by the FBI through the chief state attorney.

He once again found himself slipping to the bottom of that self-pitying pit of hopelessness and the hope of freedom he had visualized as a small ray of light far away began to diminish once again. His belief in the Universal Law of Attraction withered with that dim light.

Neil had not stopped thinking about Clarke but he was still unable to consider her as the one responsible for his detention. He was hopeful that, once the charges were filed against him, she would come to visit him but she had not shown up so far despite it being four days since he had been formally charged by the FBI.

His parents had also come to the US as soon as they were informed about their son's predicament. Thankfully, Ajay had comforted them and told them that personally, he had no doubt of their son's innocence and that he truly was not involved in any kind of cybercrime. As soon as they could help identify the real culprits, Neil would be released.

***

In the offices of Waverley Davis, Ajay and Jacob chatted. "You look really tense, Dad, what's up?"

"It's Neil," Ajay said.

"He's been charged, hasn't he?" Jacob asked. He had guessed correctly. Neil had been accused of treason.

"You always say that we must allow the law to take its own path so I think we must wait and see."

"Yes, well I'm thinking about doing some digging at our own end," Ajay said determinedly.

Well, every investigation of ours has led us to him so far and he has no answer or explanation. He could also be completely innocent and not know anything about it thought Jacob. "He's my friend Dad, I'm not liking it a bit that he's facing this crisis all by himself either. But now he's in custody that's the way it is. We'll have to wait to see how he pleads in court."

***

James, one of the investigation officers for the FBI, was sent to search an apartment in downtown New York. He reported back to the team briefing later. "There's no one there. The apartment is empty. Cleaned. Whoever was there left after removing every trace of ever having been there," James reported back to HQ in his field report from Natalie's apartment.

They, the FBI, were on Natalie's tail after forensics were able to isolate the transmit/receive unit which had led James and his squad there. "Yes sir. We've recovered it. It was planted under the top of the computer table top," James reported to Christopher's briefing about the hidden transmitter which his team had just recovered.

James was originally tasked with following the signal frequency of that transmitter and to identify anyone entering or leaving the apartment. James had previously followed the signal to the door of Natalie's apartment inside the residential building. Initially, he didn't realize that the apartment had been abandoned by its inhabitants.

One undercover operative, disguised as a mail delivery man, was also in place near Natalie's apartment to keep an eye on anyone entering or leaving the apartment. When they hadn't seen any activity for more than an hour, James instructed his undercover operative to peek into the apartment using the digital equipment that the FBI used for such operations. They inserted a small camera below the main door to look for any sign of life inside but what they saw was an absolutely empty apartment.

They forced entry and tried to find any traces of finger prints but James was stunned to see that the apartment was thoroughly cleansed and whoever had been there had gone to extraordinary lengths to get rid of every single finger print. Not the behavior of a normal person. They must be very alert, methodical and savvy of the FBI's operational procedures. They had vast knowledge of such exit procedures. Such a person could not be completely innocent. Despite being on the other side of the law, James was impressed. He had never ever seen anything like this before.

However, he did have one major concern. "What's the point of leaving a transmitter behind?" James asked Christopher once he got back to office.

"They didn't leave it. It was planted there to spy on whoever was there. That reminds me of that saying, set a thief to catch a thief. That appears to be what's happened in that apartment. And we know this for a fact, people like that are seldom innocent," Christopher said.

***

Natalie had now moved into Jenifer's apartment which was located only four blocks away from her own. Jenifer had decided to disappear once again after helping Natalie to move into her place. Together, they had moved all of Natalie's clothes, her computer and the rest of her belongings.

Jenifer was trying to understand the possible circumstances which had led to the deaths of Fu Wang and the other Chinese operatives. She had a strong feeling that they both could have avoided this whole situation had she informed the authorities or the Waverley Davis management about the proposed plan right from the start.

Natalie, sitting in the apartment, began thinking about Neil once again. Suddenly, she imagined Neil receiving the death sentence as punishment for his crimes. "My God," she thought. Her mind swirled about their current predicament. She waited for Jenifer and after few minutes turned on the TV and flicked through the channels.

Her finger stopped at a news channel where Neil's image appeared in the main news bulletin. She was devastated when she learned the nature of his charges and the consequence of him paying such a high price for someone else's crimes.

***

Jacob was once again on a dinner date with Jenifer. They made their choices after contemplating the lengthy menu. Sitting opposite, they stared at each other and touched hands as they chatted. She had not made any attempt to hack Jacob's phone despite having had many chances to do just that. When he visited the restroom a couple of times, he had left his mobile on the table with Jenifer. She would stare at it but she never once picked it up. Why she was behaving like this, even she had no idea. Somehow her feelings, when she was with Jacob, were different from how she felt when she was with Neil. She had also started to like his style of talking and dressing and his caring nature and, most importantly, his very passionate eyes.

Jenifer had been quiet since they had arrived. Jacob had asked her why but she persuaded him that everything was fine and she was just a little tired due to extra workload. She told Jacob that one of her friends had come to live with her for the next few days.

"The meal and the evening have been so perfect," he commented and continued "I could not have asked for anything better, beautiful food, superb wine and most importantly your company," he said. Just then she stood as if to leave.

"Do excuse me, I have to go to the restroom," she said. On reaching the ladies' powder room, she locked herself in one of the cubicles and put her head into her hands. She sighed and realized from Jacob's kind words what kind of feelings he had for her and what she had done to make him feel that way. Thinking things through, from what

Jacob had told her a few days earlier, she already knew that Neil was Jacob's best friend and what had happened to him. Sitting there in that darkened room, she acknowledged that she was developing a keen fondness for Jacob too. She felt that maybe she was deceiving him even though that was what she had originally intended at the beginning.

"Oh my God, what should I do?" she asked herself, "What have you done to me, Jacob?" The feeling that arose became the seed of love. Hitherto undeclared and unseen, hidden deep in her heart she could now feel it very clearly even though they had not declared their love. She sensed that Jacob was going to say those three magical words anytime and although her inner self became more unsettled by the possibility this was exactly what she wanted to happen sooner rather than later. That concealed seed of love was growing, as the mask of that indifferent sociopath called Jenifer started to be shed.

Her subconscious mind was being rewired for a change and the change in prospect disturbed her to such an extent she had gone to the restroom to seek refuge. However, the seed of change was becoming more permanent. The moment of truth was drawing near. It was nearly before her and she needed to make a difficult decision. She could pray for Neil's conviction and stay with Jacob. She had to decide whether to keep this secret safe or come clean about her role in the entire situation and leave her fate in

Jacob's hands. She could not live with this duality when she was falling for someone. She returned to the restaurant and Jacob saw her coming back, she was looking very relieved. After exchanging goodbyes, they both left the restaurant.

Jenifer had made her decision.

Chapter Eleven

There is no man living who isn't capable of doing more than he thinks he can do.

Henry Ford

There were four participants at the meeting taking place in a private room of a club with invitation only membership. The club's biggest service promise was total privacy and secrecy for all its membership. The club played host to very selective guests who came from all over the world to negotiate secret deals, sometimes even among apparent enemies if both could agree on the same agenda and goals. Others would meet and just pretend to be allies to ensure that they could keep their enemies closer, just to keep an eye on them. This meeting was a similar one as, here too, the participants had come from different worlds which, according to the daily news bulletins on TV, were described as being hostile towards each other.

Most senior among the participants was an aged former European banker and visionary business strategist, Ken Fellows. Due to his genuine political and strategic insight he had earned a very strong public and corporate reputation throughout Europe. Many European Union governments would use his advice when making strategic decisions.

He was dressed in a smart crisp two-piece suit and was wearing glasses. The meeting had been convened by the second participant, Francis Juke from the United States. The third guest was Abu Salem from the Emirates whilst the fourth participant was Anton Sergei from the Russian

FBS (Federalnaya Sluzhba Bezopasnosti Rossiyskoy Federatsii), the Russian Secret service.

The meeting began. This was a secret, high-level security brief.

Ken Fellows initiated the meeting by beginning "It seems that the Americans have not learnt anything from their past mistakes. I'm afraid if they continue to make strategic miscalculations, similar to Iraq and Libya, they could end up ruining stability in Europe again. Just look how their military intervention in the Middle East has created a serious refugee crisis for mainland Europe. The United Kingdom has left the European economic union in a recent referendum due to mass migration as a result of the pending crisis in previous war zones."

He continued, "The UK consequently cannot control its borders, the result is an exit from the EU to claw back border controls. Many consider this development to be a crisis for the future of the EU. Although I also have my concerns in this regard I think there's a possibility we can all turn this crisis into an opportunity for a much more stable future. The Americans are still living in the Post-Cold War era but with the power shift from West to East and the resurgence of Russia in the last few years, it has been made abundantly clear that a multi-polar world has emerged which means an international system cannot work with the old political dogmas anymore."

"So, Mr. Fellows, while I appreciate your remarks about the changing world and the Russian role in it, I'm still not able to see what you proposing here," Anton Sergei interjected. He continued, "I think Ken Fellows has a proposal for the longer term stability in the world particularly around all the global strategic hotspots."

Francis Juke added to the debate from the perspective of a mid-level executive in the Waverley Davis Hi-Tech Machine Department. This organization-wide department was responsible for catering for every kind of hi-tech engineering and manufacturing machine maintenance operation across all research divisions. His department was the only one in the entire company with full access to every kind of research machinery installed at Waverley Davis. Maintenance operations were controlled through computer software but these computers were not attached to the Waverley Davis network for security purposes. The network interfaces on these computers were disabled permanently and required admin access to be enabled. New machine procurement would happen on the outcome reports of this department.

"Yes, you're right, Francis. We must remember this is not an easy task to accomplish at a time when all democracies, particularly America, are being run not by any political ideology but by industrial complexes including those related to the military and the world will remain in great peril unless that changes or at least their military industrial complex start behaving differently," Ken Fellows said while looking out of window where the sun was slowly going down in the sky and London looked magnificent.

The other three participants listened to him attentively. "After reading world history and travelling across the globe, I've learned that humans have made progress only in those eras when they had listened to each other by crossing every apparent political or ideological divide. I'm British by birth. When I was very young, I saw my birth city, London, going through a massive rebuilding program after the horrors of World War II. It had been almost demolished and left in ashes."

He added, "Since then, I've witnessed humans making the same mistakes over and over again. Superpowers have monopolized our world resources for centuries. Now we are also faced with the control of knowledge itself, the knowledge we now yearn for is military and its strategy for wars which are triggered by the acquisition of global resources and the control of trade routes, the very resources which are necessary to sustain life on this planet. This is a viscous circle, doomed to failure. This is where the very fabric of democracy and nation states are being torn apart in their quest for control. This is why the silent, nameless, marginalized people all across the world are being fragmented. If we're going to stop all this, we must end this monopoly on knowledge which creates the strategic imbalance in the world. The ideal way to do that is to spread awareness and create a mass awakening but that will take lots of time, time which we just don't have."

He continued, "The North American cyber revolution goes some way to control its superior technological advantage to temporarily achieve this. Military contractors, like Waverley Davis, control the knowledge through so called 'Patent monopoly' which leads to this sense of technological superiority in the American strategic community when new war engines are created based on these patents. I'm fine with patent monopolies as long as it is some luxury item like a new smartphone chip or automated car drive module but not when it endangers humanity or involves manufacturing weapon systems. Once resources are spent on manufacturing these systems, they sell them to the Pentagon and then that becomes a business motive to maximize their profit."

He concluded his long lecture as on his feet. "This is what has transpired in the USA since the end of World War II. The world has become a stable place, not because of the United Nations, but because of the threat of Russia and the fact that there was a strategic balance in the shape of two global powers, US and USSR, to keep the world safe by keeping away from each other. After the World Trade Centre attacks, the threat of world conflict was perceived to have increased global terrorism while traditional rivalries and strategic posturing seems to have decreased.

The realms of war now hang on conjecture and hearsay, indicating another global conflict in the making. My mission today, gentlemen, is to see that that never happens. That's why we're all here together, regardless of our faith or race."

He sat down having concluded his speech.

"Your reputation of a desire for global peace precedes you Ken and we all share the same dream. Please let us know how we can contribute to the realization of this dream and make the world a better place to live," Francis Juke added. This was a brief and concise comment which did not really add anything and then Abu Salem spoke for the first time.

"Each and every one of us here has a role to play and, considering our joint international reputations, we can restore balance back into the world if we all work together. What as a group do we recommend?" He continued, "My understanding is that we're going to conduct a cyber-operation at Waverley Davis. Therefore, if I'm right, we're trying to do the same thing that the Chinese FBS failed at despite their best efforts. In particular, we have no idea what the Chinese were looking for in the first place."

"My sources in China have confirmed that even the nature of the Waverley Davis secret cyber project is not known," Anton Sergei commented.

"Well, it was a top secret revolutionary navigation system for the US Navy detection service," Ken Fellows intervened. Unsurprisingly, Anton Sergei looked puzzled.

Ken outlined the project, "It's much more than a navigational system. It's basically an advanced real-time satellite aided navigational plus tracking system which would let the US navy identify friend or foe ships in hostile oceans. This would instantly give an unprecedented advantage to the US Navy to cripple any adversary during any future naval conflict. Waverley Davis has been secretly working on this for the last two years."

"Monopolizing battlefields, humans and their insanity," Fellows added, placing an open folder on the table. "I think we now have enough understanding of the challenge we are faced with. It's time to discuss our future strategy to ensure global peace through establishing how to prevent this American project concluding." Suddenly everyone was intrigued.

Anton Sergei was thinking what possible role this deterrent would play in helping his country restore some of the former Russian glory. Abu Salem was the most perplexed amongst the four of them. He was totally unable to understand his own personal role or his country's possible role in this hi-tech game but he had been told that, for his part, he would personally receive a high financial reward from the operation. He thought about financial backing to support the militia of his chosen sect which was one of many factions fighting the sectarian wars in Iraq and Syria. This, his sectarian faction, had already killed thousands of innocent people so far.

Ken Fellows was thinking about the money he would receive from the Russians for selling the secrets of Waverley Davis. Something he had done previously as well. He did not consider it to be blood money.

He was the only person in the room who visualized a peaceful and stable world with multiple power brokers at a global level. Lots of bad karma had been earned by the other three participants. The universe absorbed it.

***

"We're no longer able to get into their network," Natalie informed Jenifer who was lost in her own thoughts, looking quite distraught as if she had lost something very valuable.

"Did you hear? I'm not able to access the backdoor you created at Waverley Davis." Natalie's eyes were glued to the computer screen then she looked towards Jenifer after waiting for couple of minutes for her reply. "What's happened? Are you OK?" Natalie asked anxiously.

"Nothing happened, everything's fine," Jenifer replied but Natalie was barely able to hear her.

"We've been kicked out of the Waverley Davis computers. You're sitting there lost to the world, without telling me the reason and now you're insisting that everything is alright. Nothing is right. Please tell me what's going on?" Natalie was seriously concerned now.

"It's ok if we're not in their network anymore. I've changed my plan. We'll be leaving here soon," Jenifer shocked Natalie who was still baffled by the whole entire situation.

"You're not a person known for having second thoughts so tell me, Jenifer, what the hell has happened?" Natalie really was curious now.

"I don't know," she replied staring out of window. "Whatever it is, I never felt anything like this before in my life. I desperately need more money but something inside me won't let me harm him in any way, shape or form."

Natalie was still struggling to connect and understand Jenifer's slow disconnected replies. Jenifer had hesitated to grasp what the missing piece of this complicated puzzle was. However, now she had the last piece, everything became clear to Natalie.

"So love happened, I guess," Natalie suggested.

"It was never supposed to happen," observed Jenifer. "All my future plans have been thrown into the air."

Seeing her in such a state was not easy for Natalie. "We're talking about Jacob, right?" Natalie asked the question whose answer was already very obvious.

Jenifer nodded her head and tears began to roll down her cheeks. Natalie embraced her, patting Jenifer's back with one hand, trying to comfort her. "You were saying something about leaving this place?" Natalie said after few minutes. "You mean that we're fleeing New York like I suggested before? Well, OK, that's brilliant, finally some peace from constantly chasing our tails." She just wanted confirmation from Jenifer.

"Yes. We'll be leaving the US in the next couple of days. I've made all the arrangements."

"When did you make all these plans?" Natalie asked.

Jenifer shocked Natalie again when she asked where they were going.

"Brazil, you know how much I love the beaches there," Jenifer explained. "Pack some light clothing and take this and keep it safe," Jenifer said, handing a large thick envelope over. Natalie took it and looked into it and was shocked to find money in it. There was thousands of dollars in cash, cool green cash.

“Where did you….” Natalie was about to ask further questions but Jenifer raised her hand and said, “No more questions.” Natalie was anxious to find out more information but she wasn’t going to get the answers today because right now Jenifer had decided to leave. She started packing.

After couple of days preparing to leave, they arrived at La Guardia airport. When they got there, Jenifer told Natalie that she would be traveling to Brazil alone. This was a tremendous shock for her of course and she tried to protest but Jenifer made her understand, after much argument, that she was sending Natalie away now only so that she could take care of the Jacob matter.

This made Natalie even more furious. She complained out loud “You could have told me about your plans,” Natalie said sharply.

“Yes, I know. I should have said something but you know how much was happening around us. Now we’ve lost Fu Wang it complicates matters even more.”

Natalie tried to put herself in Jenifer’s shoes and thought that perhaps Jenifer was telling the truth. Just then, the final call was announced for Natalie’s flight. They embraced each other and Natalie left for the departure lounge. Jenifer watched until she passed into the passenger only area. She left the airport when the Brazil flight had taken off. Soon, she was in her car driving towards the Waverley Davis Headquarters.

It was time to face the biggest demon inside her!

"I think you're here to meet Jacob, is that right?" he asked.

"No, Ajay, I'm here to meet you, actually. I should have come earlier but I think I may still have enough time left and I hope I'm not too late," Jenifer replied attempting a smile.

"Not too late for what?" he replied.

"OK, I mean not too late to finally put right this mess right," Jenifer replied now in a much more serious tone.

She continued, "There are some things I need to discuss, things that you need to know about and things that are extremely personal. You need to listen to this, it's vitally important in order to help you get rid of this hacking problem of yours. I wouldn't be taking up so much of your time if the things I want to tell you won't enable you to understand everything that's been going on lately."

Ajay was intrigued to know what this girl had to tell him and wondered, if he did listen, that she would solve the Waverley Davis network security problems.

She continue, “To start with, you should know that Neil is innocent. I implanted that malware deciphering code on his mobile.” Ajay gasped then fell into a stunned silence.

“How could this happen? You.....You are Jacob’s...” Ajay could not complete the sentence, he had no idea what to say to her.

“Let me explain to you from the beginning. You must be keen to know how this all began, aren’t you?” Ajay could only nod his head to prompt her to begin.

She then went on to explain to Ajay about her past life, her life so far in the technology sector, the difficulties of her childhood, her challenging education and how she became besotted with learning all about hacking. And then the list grew and grew and he listened as she told him about how he was her inspiration during her younger days with his teachings about the Law of Attraction.

She explained how his inspiring work had motivated her to deal with the paralysis of her mother and how his healing words had equipped her to face how her father had destroyed their family. She told him about her previous hacking exploits and finally how she got the assignment to hack into Neil’s mobile via a Chinese agent from the communist regime. She kept secret Natalie’s role in the entire story, totally excluding her from the account.

Meanwhile, Ajay remained silent and just listened but she had now reached the most difficult part of her confession. It was hard for her to tell Ajay about her initial plans for Jacob but she had already confessed to everything else. She told Ajay bit by bit about what she had actually planned to do to Jacob. Ajay kept listening to her, wondering why she hadn't fled the country already or why she hadn't walked into his office to tell him all this in the first place.

Then, "For heaven's sake, why did you come here? You could have just disappeared?" Ajay asked solemnly.

"Well," she replied, "have you ever in your life fallen in love with someone?" Ajay was certainly not expecting that answer.

Ajay was completely lost for words. He tried to fill in the missing pieces from what he had just heard, joining up the virtual dots so that he could draw a complete picture in his mind. What he knew for sure was that he was looking at the girl his son had fallen in love with and who was also responsible for Neil's detention. She had conspired with some unknown foreign elements against his company and his country.

Jenifer fell short of telling him about her role in saving the Waverley Davis server so many times from the Chinese. "It was Jacob who made me walk in here and say all this to you," she explained, "to confess to my wrongdoings. I wanted to do this in front of him but I couldn't find the courage in me for that. I wanted to tell him that I'm not worthy of his love but my conscience refused to take me to him."

"So, as a result I came to you," Jenifer talked as if she was in some kind of trance. She remembered the moment when she had made her mind up to come clean to Jacob but could not say anything to him.

Suddenly, Ajay realized there was a third person in the room. It was Jacob who had been standing there, in the doorway, for at least the last ten minutes and he had heard the last part of Jenifer's confession. Jacob was stunned to learn this about Jenifer. His body and mind both became numb and he stood there for few moments expressionless. After he had regained some composure from the initial shock, he left Ajay's office without a single word.

Ajay was bewildered by all the drama unfolding there in his office. He looked towards Jenifer who had her eyes closed, tears rolling down her cheeks. Ajay then picked up the phone to call the FBI. Just then Jenifer opened her eyes. "I think you must also be wondering about the mysterious hacker who helped your team to secure your servers and network?" she asked.

"How do you know so much detail?" he asked.

"Because I'm the one who did it, that securing on line inside your server," she confessed.

"You mean, you did all that work to save my networks?" Ajay asked. Then Jenifer told him all the details of her role in the whole story. Needless to say, Ajay was completely amazed, perplexed and confused all at the same time. He put the phone down as now he was not sure if she was an enemy or his best friend or at least his company's best friend. She decided that she was now ready to leave the building and, as she left, she said, "I think now, I must go where I belong."

When she had left his office, Ajay sat quietly and began to try to understand the entire situation that had just been played out before him. Somehow, strangely enough, just listening to Jenifer's confession he felt exactly the same way he had felt when Neil was apprehended by the FBI weeks earlier.

On her way out of the building, Jenifer spotted Jacob who looked heartbroken. Regardless of this, Jenifer decided she did not want to face him, she tried to pass him in the corridor but as she passed his office he was standing right in her way.

"Who the hell are you? You're a two-faced liar, Jenifer," he started.

"You know I would never hide anything from you. I came here today to tell the truth and I think you should have realized that by now," Jenifer said calmly.

"Why speak of this now?" he asked, anguish etched in his voice. "Why confess now?"

"You made me do this Jacob. I'm just an ordinary girl really, not a sociopathic liar."

Jacob was stunned to see tears in Jenifer's eyes and had no idea what to say. He let Jenifer pass and as soon as she had left he headed to Ajay's office. "I think we should stop her. I'm calling security." Jacob picked up the phone but Ajay stopped him.

"That will not be necessary, Son. She's going to surrender herself to the FBI soon anyway." He began to explain to Jacob, "You know, Jacob, she's your mystery hacker who saved the Waverley Davis network from the Chinese invasion time and time again."

Jacob remembered how he visualized meeting this mystery cyber friend, Hacker X, to thank him or her and now he had no idea how to react to this emerging situation.

"Well, one good thing, Jacob," Ajay said gratefully, "we now know that at least Neil will be freed from jail."

More than anything, Jacob was disgusted with himself. How could he be so stupid as to fall for that type of a girl? However, he kept thinking about her saying “You made me do it, Jacob.” This gave him something to consider within the conflict churning around in his already dizzy head.

The following morning, Jenifer surrendered herself to the FBI for her role in Neil’s case. The entire national media picked up the story and it became the hottest breaking news. The news of Jenifer’s arrest and confession in front of FBI investigators also broke on the internet. When the hacking incident became known to its investors and stakeholders Waverley Davis managed to negate any public relations damage. Like every corporate entity, Waverley Davis had an urgent contingency plan in place ready to address any uneasiness among its valuable investors. As the share price moved downward, Waverley Davis quickly issued a midterm equity share bonus, placing extra profit in the pockets of investors and stakeholders. This calmed the downslide on the NYSE Stock exchange and the shares quickly rallied. This included the Waverley Davis subsidiaries overseas whose value climbed upward equally quickly.

***

Still in London, Ken Fellows had put his plan into motion. The crafty maneuvering of Francis Juke had proved to be the most instrumental element in the execution of that plan. Abu Salem was the second most critical component after that. Though Anton Sergei's role was also important, it was those other two money hungry crooks who were playing the key roles.

Within the next few days, all three met in the middle of a desert in Syria. Syria, a country engulfed in civil war, had become the hotbed of a covert battle between various intelligence agencies operating within that theatre of war. Each of them came selfishly trying to protect the strategic interests of their respective nation states.

"So, you think we should choose this place for our launch pad?" Francis Juke enquired of the others.

"Yes, thanks to your government's foreign policy, this is the only safe place anywhere on Earth where people can operate freely, without drawing any attention," Abu Salem replied.

"But how will this work in the desert?" Francis Juke asked whilst staring at the sea of sand around him.

"In the next three days, all the arrangements will be made. All the equipment Sergei's got at the Russian airbase in Ataxia will be shifted here including those generators," Abu Salem told him.

"What about the local security?" enquired Juke? "We'll be away from the prying eyes of intelligence operatives here but you know this country is at the epicenter of religious fanatics each fighting their separate sectarian wars. How, then, can we protect our operation from them?"

Sergei spoke for the first time. "Well then, this is exactly why I've chosen this place. I was aware of your concerns because Ken told me about all the requirements for this operation."

They each acknowledged his response and after a few more minutes, they all left heading for their three different hideouts and arranged to meet again in three days' time.

***

In the West Wing of the White House, the Secretary of Defense, Robert Miller, put the file on the table after having gone through it twice. In the room with him was Major General Edward Vice, one of the highest ranking officers in US Navy Cyber Command.

"So what do you want from me, General?" the Secretary of the Defense asked.

"Your intervention and the power to drop federal charges, sir," he replied.

The General thought for a few seconds then added, "Then her inclusion in our team."

"Now that's a demanding list. Don't you think this matter needs more investigation?" asked Robert Miller.

"Mister Secretary, we're under attack. The agents from the NSA listening station reporting back to the CIA and the FBI have now just unearthed the real scope of this operation. It was, and is, a strategic operation. You know how important 'Project Xerox' is for our forces in winning in the South China Seas, Sir, and other hotspots around the globe. Projects like these are the pillars of our defense strategy and our leadership role in the world."

The Pentagon officer had come fully prepared. "I'm ready to intervene if she's as skilled as you're telling me but, and it's a big but, how much do we know about her background and any possible link to any foreign state or non-state alliance?" Robert Miller asked.

"Sir, teams from almost all of our intelligence agencies can verify her story independently and from preliminary findings vindicate her story. We'll let you have a detailed report on your table in couple of days max," the naval commander replied.

"Hmmm…. well, in that case, I can get someone working on your first request then. Charges of espionage against this country will only be dropped when I learn that she's done nothing to harm the US and has in fact helped us save Project Xerox as you mentioned in this file," Robert Miller said picking up the phone on his desk.

“Thank you very much, sir. You’ll get a positive report about her, I promise, and God bless America,” said the Major General before leaving the Secretary’s office.

***

At New York’s State Penitentiary Block C, Neil was lying on a small bed in his cell when he heard noises outside his door. He was asked to stand away from the door. He stood up and stepped back and, within a few seconds, two guards came in and beckoned him to the door.

“Congratulations, Neil,” the Sergeant said to him as Neil stepped outside his cell. “Well done, you’re going home.” Neil was still trying to process what was happening as he listened to the Sergeant’s words. He was taken to another room in the building. The clothes he was wearing when he was taken into custody were returned to him and within a few minutes he was outside the prison on the road astonished by his sudden release.

He had been facing allegations from both Waverley Davis and the US State department. He had been informed earlier that day that Waverley Davis had dropped all charges against him. He had thought that this was a futile act of empathy by Ajay. He also believed he would never be free anytime soon because he was still classed as an enemy of the State.

He needed answers and there was no better place to start than at Waverley Davis. When he reached the offices he was baffled. Jacob and Ajay and many of the employees had come out to greet him. He had never dreamed he would receive such a wonderful welcome.

"Thank you everyone," Jacob shouted to the crowd who slowly filtered away.

"God, please tell me what's been going on here?" Neil pleaded.

"I'll tell you everything, old friend, but first of all, please allow me to say how sorry we are for your detention. We knew you'd come here before going anywhere else as soon as you got released," Ajay said.

"Yeah, but please tell me something. How did I get out? Did you capture the real culprit? If so, who was he?" Neil was full of questions.

"OK big boy, get up." Jacob was pulling at Neil's arm. "We're going home now and I'll tell you everything there in full detail." They both walked out of the office.

Neil had no idea how seriously Jacob's revelations were about to shock him.

***

Jenifer was put into a cell in the prison holding area of the FBI Federal Headquarters at The Plaza Building, 23rd

Floor, Downtown, New York. She was held in the cells used for holding suspects who are awaiting investigation. She felt totally disconnected there, with no access to the outside world, whatsoever. How did the universe let all this happen? She felt sorry for herself mostly, especially as she felt weakened in reaction to her feelings. "Is love such a formidable power on Earth," she mused.

Her mind wrangling continued. If love makes people weaker, she thought, as it had indeed made her, then why in the world was she so crazy with these dark thoughts. She needed a reply. But there was no one in that cell to respond. She was, though, in the perfect environment to connect with her inner self and that was what happened.

Alone there in that cell.

Scenes from her dates with Jacob began playing vividly in her imagination. She began to remember her feelings, why she enjoyed his company and why she had initially gone out with Jacob. Then she remembered how she had felt when she had discovered the seed of love in her heart for the first time. She recalled her hours longing for Jacob's company and though how formidable love was. It is so powerful, this love thing, that it can transform anybody's personality. It is possible to simply rewire our brain to change our personality completely.

At least now she had the answers she wanted but she had become deeply disturbed after realizing that she had never had a chance to express her feelings to Jacob. The agony of wishing in her heart became palpable. Why had she not felt the power of love with this intensity before confessing her crimes? Jenifer closed her eyes and imagined herself with Jacob once again, telling him that she loved him. She could no longer visualize this without becoming sad, tears running down her face.

With every passing hour, such questions and soul searching were becoming routine for her. Then one day, she wished she could be with Jacob more permanently, so she envisioned being in his life once again. Strangely that night, she felt a mysterious kind of rush in her mind when she imagined herself with him.

Little did she know that at that moment she was not only thinking about Jacob but was also attracting him? The Law of Attraction had begun its magical manifestation.

***

Elsewhere, Jacob sat, still heartbroken, and wondered why he had deserved to be treated like this in life. He had very few friends and, after Jenifer's confession, his confidence regarding friendships had been shaken pretty badly. He had also got many questions which were the same as or similar to those that Jenifer had faced. He wanted so much to hate her but somehow he was not able to find that red mist of rage for her. This made him even more puzzled about his ability to think straight.

Unlike Jenifer, Jacob had no spiritual side and failed to establish a connection with his inner self in order to seek the answers. He needed help in that respect. He wanted some fatherly help to answer his questions so that his mind could be set free from these memories. He could not put her out of his mind even after he searched inside for a way to forgive and forget her.

He was ready to accept of spiritual help for the first time. The perfect cosmic conditions to overcome his stubborn resistance had been fulfilled.

Chapter Twelve

Thinking is the hardest work there is,

Which is probably the reason so few engage in it.

Henry Ford

It was another chaotic day in the busy Waverley Davis input server room. Victor and Farrell were both working flat out in fighting a war to keep the network secure. However, on this occasion, the attack was causing multiple waved network wide chaos. It seemed that someone or something had just crippled all the security measures and gained access to different utility servers freely.

"How the hell are they crippling our firewalls?" Victor asked with anguish. "I've never seen anything remotely like this. More importantly this looks like a military grade cyber weapon."

Victor was right in his assessment. Waverley was being hit by a Breach X9 virus, a similar strain to the virus that Jenifer had planted on Neil's mobile telephone the second time they had met. The input low level code inputs on the read out were indicating a virus payload that was calling machine level routines.

This was tricking the firewall into believing it was being interrupted in its routine and therefore the virus tricked the firewalls and other access control mechanisms in a particular way. Hence, it allowed unprotected server access.

Because of Neil's arrest on the same day it had not affected the system at that time.

Suddenly, Farrell shouted, "Oh my God, you must see this!"

"What?" asked Victor?

Victor couldn't understand what the panic was as he rushed towards Farrell's console. "What's up?" he asked and what he saw shocked him.

All the security mechanisms of Waverley Davis had somehow failed to keep the hackers out and now, for the first time, they were inside the internal firewalls.

To Victor, it was obvious that they would eventually reach the vault known as the main storage area where data about all the strategic projects was kept in encrypted form.

"This is really bad," he said.

"We must do something now," Farrell said in a panic.

"Yes, otherwise we'll be completely compromised," Victor answered quickly.

This answer caused Victor to focus on the screen, assessing the breach. This is the most sophisticated attack we've ever seen, he thought. He began to analyze the possible multiple outcomes of his failure to flush out these hackers.

"There's absolutely nothing we can do. We'll just have to let it pass and then assess the damage," he said with an element of annoyance in his voice. "It looks like the internal firewall isn't there anymore. This is a complete system crash."

Victor diagnosed the problem quickly. "The firewall is working but it's allowing the traffic. Its functionality has gone and we've no access to its interfaces. This is not how logic works. Whatever it is, it's operating on a physical layer." Victor was analyzing the attack while remembering the networking standards.

"Wait a minute. What the hell is this?!" Jacob shouted suddenly, looking at another console. Farrell and Victor were shocked to see that now the system was indicating some unauthenticated access to completely isolated network nodes. These were restricted areas of the network where servers and computers were connected with each other but had no physical connection to the main network. They were just connected to the server control room via isolated network cables.

"It's sudden death. We have no other option left," Victor said to Jacob.

"Just shut it down; everything; all of it. Cut the goddamn main supply. I don't care if the entire building plunges into darkness. Make in happen now!" Jacob shouted.

Victor rushed out of control room. He went to elevator and pressed the red button on the floor selection panel of the elevator. A prompt appeared where he entered a code and the elevator took him to the basement where the entire electrical supply infrastructure of the building was installed. Generators, with backup generators and the supply from the electricity company on a safety grid, in fact every source of energy supply to the building was there.

Victor put his hand on a palm scanner as soon as he entered the room. Everything was enclosed in a massive wired cage. There was only one small door to get through after the palm scanning. He released a sigh of relief as he realized that it least the hackers had not crippled that system.

He got inside the cage and reached the other side of the massive basement. He ran through small spaces in between various transformers, generators and supply panels. Finally he reached a steel closet and placed his head in front of it. A small retina scanner emerged from the closet and scanned Victor's retina for authentication. Once successfully completed, a keyboard tray emerged from the closet and Victor keyed in a password. The closet now opened. He could see a large LED inside indicating the power supply control software interface. He began to enter commands to instruct the system to shut down the entire power supply. He had cut the supply from the main and backup generators but the main supply from the electricity company was still on. Suddenly he lost control of the keyboard. It had become unresponsive. He instantly comprehended the situation. This system had also been hacked.

He was left with only one option. He had to do it manually. He put electrical safety gloves on and cut the main cables using a heavy axe. The entire building was plunged into darkness. No one had any idea what had happened. The only thing Victor had managed to save was the Vault. This was what Jacob and Victor thought.

The entire episode was being monitored by some very capable eyes at the US Navy Cyber Command cyber division.

***

"Sir we've lost the network access completely." one of the computer operatives shouted out loudly.

"Are you sure?" Anton Sergei asked.

"Yes, sir, I'm positive."

"Just how far did they get? Can we get into their main storage area?" Anton Sergei asked.

"We've compromised every single security mechanism there but not their main storage," the operative reported on the sabotage.

"I just hope we created enough chaos to give Ken Fellows the chance to do his part in this dark mission. If his part is now done, he'll be very happy."

"Yes, it's done. He called me himself."

"Great, now we'll see those American bastards squirm," scoffed Anton Sergei who was so happy that the final objective had been achieved.

"Allah Akbar. This is a great victory against the infidel Americans." Abu Salem was ecstatic, unaware that his actions had harmed more people of his own faith than US citizens.

***

Back in the United States, the outcome of this devastating attack was a complete public relations disaster for Waverley Davis. Thank God the US Government had intervened. The Pentagon had announced that the attack was successful only because it was unprecedented in computer history. The news had also filtered out on the internet. This international cyber debate had become the hottest topic amongst all the developed nations.

Immediately following the attack, global macro world economic think tanks and the agendas of all major world leader conferences changed. The G-7, G-20 and NATO were all told to include and discuss the issue of Cyber security in their up and coming meetings. Ajay was surprised that, contrary to his fears, everyone who mattered held sympathetic views about Waverley Davis and vowed to help overcome this world menace.

“These attacks were initiated through a European network but the origin was not in Europe. They’d used multiple hoaxes to conceal their origin.” Major General Vice was giving a briefing during a high level meeting at the White House. Ajay Mohan was representing Waverley Davis. The US Secretary of Defense, Robert Miller, was also among the small audience.

“How long will it take us to capture or kill those responsible for this attack on the US?” asked the Commandeering Chief of the USA, more usually known as the US President.

“Well, Mr. President, multiple agencies are working across the globe around the clock to bring these perpetrators to justice ASAP. We’re also in contact with all of our allies in Europe and so far we know for a fact that this attack was not initiated from any European Union country,” Major General Vice answered.

“Just how could any nation or perpetrator launch such a sophisticated attack? Is it the Russians?” the President asked again. “Maybe it’s the Chinese or the British or the Israelis?”

"Well, to be honest, sir, it could be anyone," the Secretary of Defense intervened. "Highly unlikely it's the last two, as they're are our closest allies."

The President didn't like Robert Miller's intervention.

"Sir, we'll know this in the next couple of days for sure," Major General Vice said, giving a concise answer.

"Ajay just how long will it take to resume your research work? I think you know Project Xerox has great strategic value for our nation," the President said.

"Mister President, let me break it to everyone here that the actual research work on Project Xerox was never done in the main facility office here in the US headquarters. Since the beginning, we always had the possibility of such attacks in mind. Waverley Davis and the US Navy established a top secret facility in San Francisco. As I speak, the project is almost complete. We plan to run trials in a couple of weeks after finishing the final testing of the project systems."

Nearly everyone in the meeting was pleasantly surprised apart from Robert Miller and Major General Vice.

"That's great news, very satisfactory," the US President was suddenly very excited while Jacob wondered if he would ever in his life be a physic visionary like his father.

***

Jacob had felt really disturbed since he had come back from visiting Jenifer in prison. He had gone there to confront her and to tell her that she did not have any place in his life or his heart. He had thought that this might help him cure his affliction which is what he considered his feelings for Jenifer to be. But what had transpired there had driven him senseless. He had no clue what to do. Then he decided to talk to Ajay about it. He was ready once again to receive his knowledge. "Remember, Son, you must grow more every day," his father always said, "Never stop learning."

The next day, Ajay was trying to explain to Jacob that our needs often trigger forces in the universe which are unseen, sublime yet too powerful to be overlooked. So Jacob needed to focus and realize what he wanted in life. "To understand that, consider whether you want Jenifer back in your life and focus on that question," Ajay said.

Jacob thought carefully then answered, "Well yes, of course I do, but she's a criminal and none of this makes any sense, especially not my own feelings. Why is my heart longing for a criminal?" Jacob needed an explanation for his predicament but, for the first time, he understood that life was not a linear phenomenon. You cannot think of it like any computer program.

"Let me explain," Ajay said. "First of all, she's not been convicted yet, she's only being kept in remanded for questioning. Secondly, if you consider her to be a criminal, remember that you came to know this only when she confessed to her wrongdoings. Otherwise, Jacob, she's still the same person who you would always still love to spend time with. "Remember, Son, you're only going to get what you ask for in life."

Then Jacob remembered the Henry Ford quote his Dad constantly told him.... "Whether you think you can, or whether you think you cannot, either way you think it and you are right."

"We build our life, our paradise or our hell through our thinking and then through our actions. So please remember, my son, you are going to attract everything and everyone that you wish for in your life."

***

Later, while they were having dinner that night at home Ajay said that for his part he had verified Jenifer's story and had found that she had been telling the truth, that she had acted out of desperation. "I have it verified through my various sources."

"What verified, Dad?" Jacob asked.

"Jenifer's story," he replied calmly.

"Dad, I told you, I don't want to talk about her anymore," Jacob said sternly.

"Stop thinking about her," Ajay's replied sarcastically. His answer stunned Jacob. He could say nothing because he knew his father was right. He continued to eat his dinner quietly. Again and again a rollercoaster of memories of Jenifer ran through his mind. He tried but he could not get her out of his head. Clearly his attempts were not succeeding.

"I think I need to go someplace else for few months, maybe a holiday or something."

"Well, to be honest, that's not the best idea, things will get only worse when you're all alone."

"I'm not a kid, Dad," Jacob protested.

"Then there, my son, is the problem. You're not a kid, you're a grown adult with strong emotions and even stronger memories." Jacob once again looked at his father; a person who never ceased to amaze him with his spiritual insights into his son's life.

"Dad, just how can I become spiritual like you?" Jacob asked, suddenly all childlike.

Ajay laughed. He understood what Jacob was trying to say and he was most pleased to see how much Jacob had changed.

"Well, do you think she's not a criminal?"

“Jacob! My son, you just told me that you didn’t want to talk about her anymore,” Ajay quipped, a mischievous smile on his face.

“Dad!” Jacob protested strongly. His mood was spoiled. Ajay left him sitting at the dining table and walked towards his room with a wry smile on his face.

Jacob began once again to think about Jenifer. He had realized lately that he had become completely helpless in stopping himself from thinking about her. “This is getting worse. The harder I try not to think about her, the stronger the memories become. I’ll have to get rid of these feelings. She’s a criminal,” he reasoned. Not only had she hacked into Neil’s cellphone, she’d also broken his trust. But remember she also helped Waverley Davis like no one else could, by protecting us. “Let’s be fair,” he thought.

Firstly, she had confessed to her own crimes.

Secondly, she was responsible for Neil’s arrest but she was also responsible for his release.

Thirdly, she could have cheated on you, not stayed but fled.

Lastly, she could have broken my heart but she didn’t because…. He stopped short there, but the challenging thoughts remained.

"I made her do that," Jacob muttered. "Oh My God," he uttered as soon as he realized the exact meaning of what Jenifer had said to him before her arrest. She had expressed her love in an unusual way but she had nevertheless confessed it. For the first time in many days, he was able to understand his own situation.

***

"Here it is," Ken Fellows said then tossed a USB stick towards Anton Sergei as soon as he entered the tent in the desert.

"Is it the design?" Anton Sergei asked anxiously.

"Don't think that you're that lucky, Anton," Ken Fellows said with a smirk on his face.

"The original specification wasn't there. No one knew, only Ajay knew where they were making it," Ken said and Anton Sergei was amazed.

"So what is it then?" Anton asked.

"Patience, my dear friend," he replied. "It's part of the patent research on that secret project, Project Xerox," Fellows said proudly. "I think you Russians have the resources and skills to make it work from here on in," he added.

"I think that's why the Chinese failed to find anything there," Anton said.

"The Chinese were not even close to finding it. They'd no idea what they were looking for. Waverley Davis is a vast space in the cyber world. It's not easy for anyone to find something unless he has very specific knowledge," Ken Fellows rightly said. "So when will I get paid?" he added this question at the end.

"Right now, if you want it," Anton Sergei said with a smile on his face.

"So you'll wire it now. Well, I think that would be one good use of one of these computers here," Fellows said laughing with his back turned to Anton. He was looking at the computers they had used to launch the devastating cyber-attack on Waverley Davis that had provided the opportunity for Fellows to get to one of the archive servers and grab a copy of the original patent on which Project Xerox had been designed.

The second Ken Fellows turned around to ask Anton to initiate the wire transfer. He saw the flash of a gun in Anton's hand.

"What the hell?!" Fellows yelled. "No please…" he called but Anton shot him with three point blank rounds in the chest. Ken Fellows had in fact, died instantly and as soon as he fell on the spot. Anton checked by ensuring that there was no pulse. There was no sign of life. He put the gun back in its holster and calmly walked out of the tent.

A few minutes later, a Russian military helicopter picked him up.

Ken Fellows' dead body lay there in the desert. He had reached the end he had created for himself by attracting negative bad karma.

Once again, the Law of Attraction had exactly delivered.

***

It was just another noisy night in the New York State prison for Jenifer when a guard told her that a new public defender was there to meet her to discuss new developments in her case. She wondered, why change the tactics of her defense solicitor? She had already made it clear to them all on the last visit that she was going to plead guilty in court in the upcoming hearing of her case. What the hell do they want now and more importantly, she wondered, why would any lawyer come to visit her at this hour of night. Something was not quite right. She saw a young slim woman in a smart black suit sitting on one side of table. She wore sunglasses to cover her eyes. She was black haired, tall with an athletically built body. "A new phase of this game," Jenifer thought and sat on the seat adjacent to the table.

"You're not a lawyer," she said as soon as she looked at the face of her guest.

“Impressive,” the other woman said while she pretending to search some papers in the file she held in her hand. Jenifer realized she was someone trained to show no emotion or shock.

“It’s common sense. No lawyer would come to visit a client in the middle of the night. Who are you by the way?” Jenifer was mystified by the woman who was not a lawyer but who was pretending to be.

“What else you can tell about me?” the woman asked, ignoring Jenifer’s taunt.

“You’re from a military background or some private mercenary contractor, trained in hand-to-hand combat.” Jenifer had noticed a small bruise on the other woman’s left hand.

“Not bad, I must say,” she praised Jenifer.

“And you’re a hard lady to find but then that’s common among all good hackers,” she said to Jenifer.

“What do you want at this hour?” Jenifer asked, becoming unnerved by all this drama.

“I’m here to get you out of here,” she replied with a smile. Jenifer was amazed to hear those words.

“So, she’s there to get me out,” she thought.

“Who would do that and why?” Jenifer asked the stranger, even more perplexed.

“Because my employer wants you to be on his side,” came the calm reply.

“Then tell me which side of law your employer is on?” Jenifer asked immediately. The other woman was clearly not expecting the rapidity of Jenifer’s response.

“On the right side,” she answered, “my employer is the only one who can drop all the charges against the state for you. I think now you know who my employer is or can work it out at least.” The woman then handed over some papers for Jenifer to read.

“Go through it,” she said, “and these conditions will be our terms. If you can accept them, then you will be out of here in less than twelve hours.” Jenifer began to read the papers, taking less than two minutes to go through them.

“Pen please,” Jenifer stretched out her hand. The woman smiled and handed her a pen from her pocket.

“A wise choice,” she said and walked out of the room. Jenifer was taken back to her cell.

***

It was Major General Vice who had sent one of his lieutenants to talk to Jenifer and present her with an offer for her release. As a result of accepting those terms and conditions, Jenifer had put her future in the hands of fate.

Without Jacob, every place was the same for her.

She faced a real personal crisis when she was told that Jacob was there to see her. She was desperate to see him but not like this, not under these circumstances.

Jacob had come to meet her after battling his own conscience. He wanted equally to tell Jenifer that he would be leaving her and she must forget him as well.

Both wondered how to end it.

“Hello Jacob,” she initiated the conversation.

“Hey you there,” Jacob replied, “I wanted to tell you something,” and Jenifer’s heart missed a beat. “Is he thinking the same way I have been thinking here in the prison,” she thought.

“I want to move on with my life.” Jenifer’s heart sank into a deep abyss of disappointment on earing Jacob’s words.

“OK. What’s the matter then? I thought you could have done that by now,” she said quietly after hearing about his wish to move on with his life.

“You’re the matter,” he said. “Memories of you are the matter,” he added. “Not being able to stop myself from thinking about you is the problem,” he concluded.

"You're not alone in this inferno of thoughts," Jenifer said. Jacob was stunned but stayed quiet. He was still recovering from the shock of his own unintended, confession in front of her.

"How's Neil?" Jenifer had to muster up a lot of courage to ask him that question.

"How he would be after what you did," Jacob replied. To that, Jenifer had no answer.

"I wish I could tell him how sorry I am, for doing that stupid thing," Jenifer commented to break the silence

"She was with me when I hacked into Neil's mobile. We worked together but she never met him nor did she do anything with Waverley Davis. She tried to keep me away from all of this mess. Jacob, I'm so sorry, I was worried about my Mom." Jenifer's voice broke with sorrow and, despite his strong resolve, Jacob or felt sorry for her.

Jacob noted the number of the relevant mobile. He wanted to say something to Jenifer but was unable to find any more words. Jenifer also felt the same. Both had decided not to reveal that inferno of thoughts because both were embarrassed. Jacob was ashamed that he had let words out of his mouth which exposed his true feelings for Jenifer. She was tormented by her predicament and bore the burden of all her crimes on her conscience.

Chapter Thirteen

To do more for the world than the world does for you,
that is success.

Henry Ford

An US military convey was hurtling through the desert after drifting away from its route on a major road in Syria. There were five open top military Range Rovers and one combat vehicle in that convey. It was around dusk. Commander Nathan was leading this assault to apprehend or kill a high value target. He wanted to reach their marked site before complete darkness set in and was told that his time window was closing fast.

“How long left?” he asked someone on the other side of the communication channel as it crackled its reply.

“You’re not far from target but you must hurry. They could leave the zone at any moment.”

“OK,” he shouted back, fixing his eyes on the desert terrain outside.

After a few minutes, the vehicles circled around a big tent that was camouflaged in khaki brown. Nathan’s team took their positions around the tent while he went along with one other unit to close in on the main tent. It was completely dark by now. Just as they were about to enter the tent, all hell broke loose. They were attacked by insurgents from multiple directions with all kinds of small weapons fire including RPGs, sniper fire, mortars etc. Many of the soldiers in Nathan’s team were taken by surprise amid the ferocity of this intense ambush and were killed.

“Control, we’ve been pinned down pretty bad here. We need immediate close air support!” Nathan shouted into the microphone attached to his helmet while returning fire fanatically in the dark.

This entire raid and subsequent situation was being monitored on big screens in the operational control room of the Pentagon. Two Apache helicopters were diverted to assist Nathan and his team. Drones were already in the theatre but because of a greater number of kill zone Hellfire missiles, they were not being used. Nathan and his squad were trying to fight while keeping an eye on that big tent. Suddenly, he realized that no one had fired a single shot from inside the tent and no one had come out of it either.

“Sir, we’re running low on firepower!” suddenly one of his team members shouted.

“Only use thermals. Only shoot something that you can see through your scopes. Reduce suppressing fire. If we can’t hit them from here, we’re not in their line of fire,” he instructed his men.

Within minutes, he could hear the sound of two hovering Apache helicopters some distance away. They were there in three minutes, the tables had been instantly turned and as they opened fired, all the insurgents were eliminated. Nathan and his men stormed the tent and found four critically wounded men inside. The camera on his helmet was relaying everything live to the Pentagon Control Unit where the entire situation was being assessed. Nathan was asked to identify the primary target and tried to save all four lives.

He was ordered to confiscate everything there and get his unit to send it to the nearest US Air Force Base from where it was to be shipped back to the US.

Quite quickly, one wounded person was airlifted. It was Anton Sergei. He had two serious bullet wound injuries, one in his left leg and the other in his chest. Nathan and his team left the desert after loading everything they had found in the tent including the other three wounded persons.

The raid had been carried out by a unit of US Navy Seals to capture a Russian spy who had played a key role in the latest major cyber-attack on the US. His involvement was unmasked by the capture of another insurgent who was interrogated in Syria by the CIA. He was one of the original four. It was Abu Salem who was now working against the insurgent groups backed by the United States. During his interrogation he was offered freedom if he could lead the US military to a specific target. He gave up Anton Sergei in an instant and told them about his future plan which included a similar cyber-attack on the Pentagon.

This information caused serious panic and major misgivings within the US military leadership. They had seen what BreachX9 had done to the Waverley Davis network.

Abu Salem was released by CIA after he promised that he would become a federal agent informant and that he would lead them to other targets as well. However, as soon as he was released, he leaked information about the US military raid on the operation in the open desert. This would be an ideal scenario for insurgents to catch US soldiers in open desert territory. He was correct in his tactical thinking but the insurgents failed because of one serious miscalculation; they had ignored the massive aerial firepower of the US Air Force.

The life of Anton Sergei was saved against all the odds thanks to the tremendous efforts of US military doctors. He disclosed the role of Ken Fellows in their last attack. The US leadership was disgusted to learn that the patent of Project Xerox had been compromised. The CIA recruited Anton Sergei as one of their agents within FBS and he was tasked to recover the original patent and replace it with a fictitious one. The patent switch task was successfully completed by Anton Sergei two months later.

***

"Could you ever forgive her?" Ajay asked Neil about Jenifer.

“Is that what you really think? Should I forgive her, do you think she’s worthy of my forgiveness?” Neil asked.

“You see, I am not asking for her sake but yours,” he replied. “A wise man once taught me that we cannot live in harmony and peace if we cannot forgive others and ourselves. A person who always thinks about taking revenge on others remains in perpetual pain.”

As Ajay spoke, Neil continued to look at him. His mind was trying to process what Ajay had just told him. No person prior to that had ever explained to him why ‘letting go,” was so important for us all.

“Neil, forgiveness is among the biggest virtues, the greatest source of good karma. Every time we forgive someone we earn grace, it is priceless,” he said. “We pay for our mistakes and other wrongdoings by forgiving. Please, try to understand this in the broader context. I’m not implying anything about you. If we haven’t done anything wrong to any other person, Nature gives us a second chance for any potential mistake we might made in future. Similarly, when we forgive anybody, we give him a second chance,” Ajay said. Neil could not disagree. His education from Ajay had begun once again. He did not say anything. Ajay looked at Neil’s face. He was clearly trying to reach on a conclusion.

"Remember, Neil, grace is essential in The Law of Attraction. Think about it but after disconnecting from this place," Ajay said.

Neil could not understand what he was being asked to do. I don't get it he thought, "Disconnecting from this place," he repeated Ajay's words with some astonishment.

Ajay smiled. He put an envelope down on the table and asked Neil to take it. Neil picked it up, inside was an air ticket to Brazil with hotel accommodation as well. He had always wanted to visit Brazil; it was a pleasant surprise for him. Ajay got out of his seat and wrapped both his arms around him. Neil was the only person in Waverley Davis, other than Jacob, that afternoon. "Here, you must call this number," he said, and handed the cell phone number to copy into Neil's mobile memory chip.

"Whose number is this?" Neil asked.

"Go to Brazil and see yourself. She's someone I know. Hopefully, you'll love her company," Ajay said. Neil left for Brazil the next day, a tourist destination which he had always wanted to explore.

Jenifer's plan for Teresa, had worked perfectly.

She had sent her there knowing that Neil would love to go to Brazil on vacation. Then, she had given Teresa's number to Jacob and asked him to tell Neil to call her. Jacob knew full well that Neil would never call that number if knew it had come from Jenifer. So he took Ajay into his confidence and they hatched a plan to send Neil there.

Neil and Teresa found each other.

They became friends instantly but becoming lovers took them a little bit longer.

***

Jenifer was moved to a secure location from her cell. This was not freedom but a transfer she had agreed to. She had listened to Jacob. He wanted to move on with his life. Jenifer was a hurdle for him. “Perhaps this transfer will help us both to move on with our lives,” she thought stepping into one of the black SUVs that was there to pick her up the night after she had agreed to the terms of her new employer.

She was taken to a secret training ground where Major General Vice and a female officer, the one who had visited her in prison, were there to receive her. She saw a few armed military men around as well and she was not surprised by this environment. She had expected all this during his transfer from prison.

“Welcome Ms. Jenifer Robertson,” Major General Vice said.

“What is this place?” Jenifer asked.

“Before answering your question, let me please ask you one first,” Vice said.

“OK. Ask away.”

“Do you really want to take this job, because once you’ve confirmed you do, you’ll be owned by the US Navy. We’ll tell you where to go and where not to go. What to say online and what not to say. We will…” Jenifer intervened.

“Yes, Officer, I do want to take this job. Once assigned, I take my work very seriously. So don’t worry, I’ll follow every command of yours. Just tell me where I can start working and who my target is,” Jenifer said hurriedly. Vice was taken aback and the female office tried hard to suppress a smile.

“That’s not how the US military operates. First you’ll be trained so that you can adopt our standard operating procedures and understand our way of working. We’re here to secure our homeland, not to destroy others,” the female officer had spoken for the first time. Her name was Lieutenant Lisa Starbuck.

"OK. So when are we going to start training?" Jenifer asked.

"Right now, after completing some more paperwork," Lt Starbuck replied with a warm smile. She took Jenifer into an office then, after some formalities were completed, she was shown to her room which was just a little bigger than her prison cell but a lot more cozy. She jumped on the bed as soon as Lisa left. She wanted to fall asleep but as soon as she closed her eyes, Jacob's face emerged in her mind.

"Not again. Not now," she muttered. This was not the first time this had happened to her.

She jumped out of bed and start doing push-ups on the ground. She had discovered this method of making herself tired through an aggressive workout helped her to sleep without thinking about Jacob. But even this method was not one hundred percent perfect. It worked that night and she slept tight.

Jacob was not able to sleep that night either. He wondered what had happened to Jenifer. He had gone to visit see her again the following morning but was told that there was no one with that name there, at least not anymore. He had left the prison with his head spinning.

As he left, a senior policeman told him that she had been moved to some other place by the USA military authorities but he had no idea where. Jacob just wished that he could see her one more time.

***

Some months later, Jacob was representing Waverley Davis at a military conference and exhibition. Senior military leaders, foreign delegates, foreign services chiefs and ambassadors were there from all over the world. Waverley Davis had a large booth there presenting a vast array of military solutions and hardware applications.

It was the final day of the exhibition and Jacob had been really busy meeting with delegates. He had asked Ajay to join him so that they could meet more people and secure some promising more orders. Ajay had fulfilled his son's request and had also come along. The US Army and Air Force chiefs had already visited their booth. Soon Jacob announced that the Chief of Naval Staff would also be visiting their stand. He was excited as the US Navy was the biggest customer of Waverley Davis.

Ajay received the CNS of the US Navy and started to brief him. Many senior officers accompanied the Naval Chief. Jacob was standing a few rows back to give room to the guests. That was when he heard his name spoken by a voice which he could recognize in millions of voices. He froze but had to turn around when he heard his name once more, a little louder this time but not too loud to attract the attention of others. He turned around and there she was. Jenifer.

It took Jacob a few moments to recognize her. She had a slight smile on her face. As soon as Jacob recognized her, she started to walk away from the Waverley Davis both towards a less crowded corner of the conference hall. Soon she was behind a giant advertising stand. Jacob walked behind her like he was in some kind of trance. Soon both were standing in front of each other, quiet. Not saying anything, perhaps waiting for the other to say something first.

“OK, why not just tell it like this,” Jenifer thought as she grabbed Jacob and planted a big kiss, wow smack bang on his lips. Jacob was not ready for this assault but as soon as he realized what her intentions were, he gave in and responded to Jenifer’s kiss.

“Please tell me more,” he said because now Jacob wanted to know everything that had happened to her. Why and how are had she come to be in the in the Forces. “I love you, Jacob.” Jenifer had not even listened to those other questions and said those three magical words he had waited for such a long time to him right there.

“I love you too, Jenifer.” The reply came from the depth of his heart and he kissed her once again.

"I have to go now, duty calls. I'll let you know everything as soon as I visit New York next week during my monthly leave," she said. Grabbing a pen from Jacob's pocket, she wrote her number on his hand.

"Wait, I want to know now," Jacob could say this much before he received another passionate kiss from Jenifer.

"You know, I'm too important to them and my absence will be noticed if I stay a minute more here with you and I don't think Waverley Davis can afford another scandal like this either," she said. Jacob stood there having serious doubts about the reality of space and time around him. He had craved for everything that had happened during the last ten minutes behind that advertisement stand but he had never imagined that it would happen so sudden and so unexpectedly.

Both were together once again a week later. Jenifer told him about her agreement with the State and then her inclusion in US Navy's Cyber Command. She told him how she had met with an entirely different breed of human being in the naval services who inspired her, gave extraordinary courage and confidence to her and most importantly taught her the meaning of cherishing life as long as she was alive. It was being in that company that had changed her life. She learned how to be positive under any circumstances and how to fight for good together.

Then she shared her experiences of getting clues and signs that she would be with him eventually. Jacob was amazed to hear this, as it had also happened to him but he had ignored the feelings considering them to be the result his overthinking about her. Now both understood that actually they were holding two ends of a string called love, whenever one of them pulled his end, the one holding the other end always felt it.

They remained together until Jenifer left for San Francisco where she was posted but, before she left, Jacob gave her most beautiful surprise of her life.

Jenifer had no idea what Jacob and Ajay had planned for her when she received a call from Jacob asking her to visit the Waverley Davis offices because there was some indications that a similar attempt was being made on their network again by Chinese hackers. She felt duty bound and rushed to the Waverley Davis building with the intention of assessing the situation and then reporting her findings. But once she stepped into the building she could not believe what she saw.

The entire building was decorated for some party. A massive banner read "Happy Birthday Jenifer," but no one was there. She was trying to fully understand this surprise when she heard the crowd singing a birthday song for her and Jacob emerged from his office and walked towards her. Kissing her, he suddenly went down on one knee brought out a ring and proposed to Jenifer. She was stunned and flattered but said yes instantly. They married soon after and finally Jenifer and Jacob became each other's forever. All thanks to the Law of Attraction.

Jacob took over control of Waverley Davis which continues to prosper under his masterful tutelage and his spiritual vision.

A month after their marriage, Ajay left Waverley Davis and retired to India where he wanted to visit his native town of Tiruvannamalai. He had a wish to see his native homeland once again and to spend some time in those spiritual lands and find the sanctuary he had always missed in the busy life of Manhattan.

He yearned for and got a peaceful life, a spiritual life;

All this thanks to the Law of Gratitude.

Made in the USA
Monee, IL
05 November 2026

68061790R00163